Carol Baxter is a full-time wri̶ ̶ ̶ ̶ ̶ ̶ ̶ ̶ ̶ ̶ ̶ ̶̶, ̶ ̶ ̶ ̶ ̶ ̶̶. ̶ ̶ ̶̶. She began tracing her family history while she was still at high school and, out of it, came four different career paths. She worked as project officer for the Australian Biographical and Genealogical Record and later as general editor of the Biographical Database of Australia. In these roles she edited many volumes of early colonial transcriptions. For her contributions to genealogy, she was voted a Fellow of the Society of Australian Genealogists in 2001. While writing a family history she discovered the story of a colonial sex scandal and wrote the tale as 'popular history'. It was picked up by one of Australia's top publishers, Allen & Unwin, and published in 2006. She has now completed her sixth popular history. She writes genealogical 'how to' books and gives seminars on writing and researching at genealogical conferences on land and on international cruise ships. She is also an adjunct lecturer at the University of New England, New South Wales.

Praise for Carol Baxter's 'popular history' books:

'Totally irresistible.' (*Independent*, UK)

'As lively and readable as a crime novel.' (*The Times*, London)

'A fascinating history, mystery and portrait of a complex, contradictory man.' (*Daily Mail*, UK)

'A fascinating reconstruction of a real historical case ... You can't beat a good courtroom scene, and the 50-page account of Tawell's trial is as good as any I've read in a crime novel.' (*Independent on Sunday*, UK)

'A deftly woven tale.' (*Maclean's Magazine*, Canada)

'A stellar job.' (*Publishers Weekly*, International)

'Fascinating.' (*Library Journal*, USA)

'As gripping and readable as any crime novel, but all factual and based on remarkable research.' (*Sydney Morning Herald*, Australia)

'Carol Baxter is doing for Australian history what our athletes are doing for sport: making it exciting, interesting and world class.' (*Good Reading*, Australia)

'Compelling.' (*Canberra Times*, Australia)

Also by Carol Baxter:

Popular history/true historical crime

An Irresistible Temptation (Allen & Unwin, 2006)

Breaking the Bank (Allen & Unwin, 2008)

Captain Thunderbolt and His Lady (Allen & Unwin, 2011)

The Peculiar Case of the Electric Constable (Oneworld, 2013)

Black Widow (Allen & Unwin, 2015)

Chubbie Miller (Allen & Unwin, 2017)

Genealogical 'how to' publications

Writing Interesting Family Histories (2009, 2010, 2016)

Help! Historical and Genealogical Truth: How do I separate fact from fiction (2014)

Help! Why can't I find my ancestor's surname? (2015)

Writing and Publishing Gripping Family Histories (2016)

Genealogical Guides

Guide to Convict Transportation Lists (Unlock the Past, 2015): Part 1: 1788-1800 & Part 2: 1801-1812

Edited publications

General Musters of NSW, Norfolk Island & Van Diemen's Land 1811 (ABGR, 1987)

General Muster of NSW 1814 (ABGR, 1987)

Musters and Lists: NSW & Norfolk Island 1800-1802 (ABGR, 1988)

Musters of NSW & Norfolk Island 1805-1806 (ABGR, 1989)

General Muster and Land & Stock Muster of NSW 1822 (ABGR, 1989)

General Muster List of NSW 1823, 1824, 1825 (ABGR, 1999)

Convicts to NSW 1788-1812 (SAG, 2002, CD-ROM)

Writing and Publishing

GRIPPING

Family Histories

Carol Baxter

The History Detective

First edition 2016
Copyright © Carol Baxter 2016

Carol Baxter
The History Detective
10 Melaleuca Dr, St Ives NSW 2075, AUSTRALIA
Email: c_baxter@optusnet.com.au
Web: www.carolbaxter.com

Baxter, Carol.
Writing and Publishing Gripping Family Histories.

ISBN 978-1535377843

1. Genealogy – Authorship. 2. Genealogy – Handbooks, manuals, etc. I. Title.

929.1

Printed and bound by Charles Sturt University, Bathurst.
Cover design by Alerrandre of fiverr.com.

Contents

This book is dedicated to you, the future author and publisher of a gripping family history, so that readers may not say of your work what was said of another in years gone by:

In view of the labour which has gone to the compiling of this heavy volume it is with true regret that we must record our belief that we have here a book published in haste to be repented of by its author when he shall have become more familiar with his material.

Oswald Barron *Family History in a Hurry*

Introduction

One of the best pieces of writing advice I ever received was after I handed my first 'popular history' manuscript to my publisher at Allen & Unwin. She said that it was too long and needed cutting and, to assist me, she added, 'Take off your historian's hat and put on your story-teller hat. You are now a story-teller.'

Allen & Unwin is one of Australia's top five publishing houses and my in-house publisher, whose genre covers popular history, law and politics, is now its editorial director. If *she* doesn't know what appeals to the reading public, who does?

Like most genealogists who will read this publication and its predecessor, *Writing Interesting Family Histories*, I had no official training as a genealogist, historian or writer. Like you, I began my journey because of my interest in family history research. I started tracing my family history during high school, a hobby that led to my genealogy career as project officer of the Australian Biographical and Genealogical Record and later as general editor of its twenty-first century incarnation, the Biographical Database of Australia.

Like most of you, I had no academic history training. My university major was in linguistics, of all things. However, in 2011, courtesy of my contributions to genealogy (via my edited publications) and to Australian history (via my mainstream books), I was appointed an adjunct lecturer at the University of New England, New South Wales, and remain so to this day.

And like most of you, I had never attended any classes or read any books on writing before I posted my first manuscript to Allen & Unwin. My entire writing experience, apart from university essays, lay in writing family histories and the occasional article for genealogy journals.

So what did I do that led to my mainstream 'popular history' writing career?

I broke the rules.

It was easy to do because I hadn't been taught them. In fact, I didn't discover until much later that I *had* broken the rules.

My 'rule-breaking' epiphany occurred in 2005. I had dragged myself away from writing my first manuscript to take washing off the clothes-line and was still immersed in the world of 1820s colonial Australia and the sex scandal that rocked the colony. As I stood there unpegging the clothing, I started to feel that there was something wrong with the manuscript. As clothing landed in the washing basket, I realised what it was. My story was reading – in a visual sense – like a documentary. It was as if a narrator was standing at the front of the screen in full focus telling the viewer what was happening. The protagonists themselves were at the back of the screen and were slightly out of focus. The viewer could see what they were doing, but not clearly. And the viewer could tell that they were speaking, but their voices were muted. All the viewer could hear were the intrusive words of the narrator.

In that moment I realised that, for the best reading experience, the narrator needed to be booted from the screen to allow the reader to engage directly with the protagonists. The reader needed to be able to hear what the protagonists were saying and to experience, as if first-hand, what they were doing.

In that moment I unwittingly discovered the three things that were critical for my writing success: writing history in the active voice narrative rather than the usual passive voice narrative; story-telling; and the writers' mantra 'show don't tell'. I touched on these subjects in *Writing Interesting Family Histories* and explain them in more detail in the following pages.

It usually takes six to nine months to receive a rejection letter from a publisher. I received a phone call from Allen & Unwin, the only publishing house I approached, only two weeks after posting the manuscript. That story became *An Irresistible Temptation* (2006). I have just completed my sixth book, the second to be published internationally. These days, I don't have to find the stories I write about. My publisher is finding them for me. And there is a strong chance that this latest story will end up on the silver screen.

There are many people around the world teaching genealogists how to write family histories. Most of these teachers are writing only for themselves, or for the self-published or e-book markets, or for small independent publishers. I don't know of any other family history writing teacher who is writing mainstream-published history – let alone gripping history – for the international market. And, because my own publishing break-through came about because I broke the rules, my suggestions tend to be different to those offered by other family history writing teachers. But, as is clear from the reviews on the first page, my strategies work.

My aim in this publication and in its companion volume, *Writing Interesting Family Histories*, is to teach genealogists how to rethink the way they tackle family history writing in the same way that I rethought popular history writing. The big difference is that my learning process was hit-and-miss, seat-of-the-pants stuff whereas I can now provide six mainstream-published books of tried-and-trusted examples.

In the following pages, I have mostly drawn examples from my own writing for a few simple reasons:

1. There are no copyright issues.
2. They are much easier to find.
3. I know what I began with, research-wise, and what I was trying to achieve.

I hope these suggestions prove extremely helpful.

My very great thanks to Stephen Ehat for editing and proof-reading this publication and for his assistance with my newsletters and other publications. You're a gem!

And to those whose research or writing has been drawn upon for this publication, my thanks – or my apologies.

Part 1: Writing

Either write something worth reading
or do something worth writing.

Benjamin Franklin

1

Prose Timelines

I was shocked – yet not surprised – to once read that the literary world judges the family history genre as the 'worst genre of writing'. The memoir genre reportedly came a close second.

An editor aptly summed up the problem with memoirs:

> Like most amateur memoirs, this book may be best appreciated by the writer, not the reader.

Ugh!

Replace 'memoirs' with 'family histories' and we have the problem in a nutshell. Most so-called family histories are merely attempts by genealogists to document their research and are usually fact-focused and tedious. It's as if these authors have worked extremely hard to ensure that they have sapped every last ounce of life-giving blood from their ancestors' remains. No attempt is made to bring their ancestors to life or to find their beating hearts. No attempt is made to walk in their ancestors' footsteps and see the historical context of their everyday lives and social environment. No attempt is made to use their stories to offer insight or enlightenment for the reader.

In fact, most of these publications are not 'family histories' as such. They are merely *prose timelines*.

Let me begin by explaining what prose timelines are and why they generate boring family histories. That way, we can finish with this topic in the first chapter and get on with discussing how to write gripping family histories in the following chapters.

Prose timelines
I stumbled across a classic prose timeline while researching *Black*

Widow. I googled the name of Reverend Charles Rich, who attended Louisa Collins before her execution, and found the perfect 'how not to' example for this publication.

Most of the fifth paragraph of Charles' biography is printed below (without attributions for the sake of the author):

> He was listed in a directory dated from 1866 to 1867 as Rev Charles Rich 140 Waterloo Street, Sydney. In 1866 no number was given.. (sic) He was listed in a directory dated from 1868 to 1870 as Rev Charles A Rich 147 Dowling Street, Sydney. Charles was appointed a Minor Canon of St Andrew's at Sydney, New South Wales, Australia, in 1869. Charles was the incumbent of S tBartholomews (sic) at Pyrmont, New South Wales, Australia, from 1869 to 1878. He was listed in a directory dated from 1871 to 1883 as Rev Charles Rich 128 Palmer Street, Sydney. He was listed in a directory dated from 1885 to 1887 as Rev C H Rich 'Elamang', Elizabeth Street, Paddington, New South Wales. He was listed in a directory dated between 1888 and 1889 as Rev Canon Charles Rich 'Esmond', Point Piper Rd, Padd.

So what is wrong with the above information? Let's split it into individual numbered sentences to make it easier to analyse.

1. He was listed in a directory dated from 1866 to 1867 as Rev Charles Rich 140 Waterloo Street, Sydney.
2. In 1866 no number was given..
3. He was listed in a directory dated from 1868 to 1870 as Rev Charles A Rich 147 Dowling Street, Sydney.
4. Charles was appointed a Minor Canon of St Andrew's at Sydney, New South Wales, Australia, in 1869.
5. Charles was the incumbent of S tBartholomews at Pyrmont, New South Wales, Australia, from 1869 to 1878.
6. He was listed in a directory dated from 1871 to 1883 as Rev Charles Rich 128 Palmer Street, Sydney.
7. He was listed in a directory dated from 1885 to 1887 as Rev C H Rich 'Elamang', Elizabeth Street, Paddington, New South Wales.

8. He was listed in a directory dated between 1888 and 1889 as Rev Canon Charles Rich 'Esmond', Point Piper Rd, Padd.

Problems with prose timelines

Using Charles Rich's biography as an example, let's discuss the major problems with prose timelines.

List-like nature

Rich's biography is a prose-timeline because it reads like a list of facts set out in chronological order. As shown above, it is actually easier for readers to absorb this type of information if it is displayed as a list rather than being written as prose. Of course, timelines have their uses, as shown on the next page. However, they are not suitable for the broader audience that a family history book embraces.

Family history readers do not want to be hammered by facts. They want to immerse themselves in the world of their ancestors. The only genuinely interesting family histories – the type that family history readers truly want to read – are written as *narratives*.

Sometimes family historians add chunks of historical context between the chronological entries, as is discussed further in chapter eight. These are still prose timelines albeit of a slightly better quality.

Documentation of event

Charles' biographer repeatedly writes 'He was listed in a directory dated from ...' because he is describing the documentation of an event rather than the event itself. This is an extremely common occurrence in prose timelines (discussed further in chapter three).

In fact, the source of Charles' biographical information should NOT be included in the body of his biography. What is important is what the information tells us: that Charles moved house. Yet at no point does the author specifically state that the changes in Charles' directory listings are signs of his residential relocation. Sure, we can assume that that's what the author intended to communicate. But a *biography* is supposed to communicate a person's life story not list the sources. This is another critical difference between gripping family histories and boring prose timelines.

And so on ...

There are many other problems with Rich's prose timeline: location anchoring, naming usage, source referencing, abbreviations and errors. These are discussed in chapter eighteen.

Embrace our timelines

Prose timelines are boring because they fail to tell the *story* of a person's life. They merely list the *facts* about a person's life. And, as shown above, attempting to transform a timeline into prose doesn't mask the fact that it merely lists the facts.

That doesn't mean that timelines are not useful. In fact, they are essential if we want to write a gripping narrative. My recommendation is to produce a clear-cut timeline for each of our biographical subjects, with appropriate annotations, which is published at the end of our subject's biography or at the end of the family history.

Some of the above information from Charles Rich's biography is used below to show how we can produce these types of timelines (covered in more detail in *Writing Interesting Family Histories*). All the facts and source-references are included and can be easily accessed by researchers who want to examine the sources for themselves.

Timeline for Reverend Charles Hamor Rich

1829 Jun 26	Born at Camberwell, Surrey, England[1]
1833	Arrived Sydney, New South Wales, Australia[2]
1866-7	Residing at 140 Waterloo Street, Sydney.[3]
...	

Sources
1. Baptism, Camberwell Parish, Surrey: Charles Hamor Rich ...
2. ...

If we decide to include annotated timelines in our family histories, we know that every fact about our ancestors is documented and is easily accessible by other researchers and writers. We no longer need to include every little detail in the body of our narrative. This allows us to release our creative writing spirits to produce more interesting – if not gripping – family histories.

2

The three-legged stool

A few years ago, I had another writing epiphany. I realised that the phrase 'family history' tells us the three components we need to write a gripping family history. These are:

1. Family
2. History
3. Story

Most genealogists fail to include all three components in their family histories. Their importance is explained below.

1. Family

A family history documents the lives of a number of family members, usually multiple generations of a blood-related family. Most list the basic birth, marriage and death details for the family members along with spouses, children, occupations and residences.

Many family histories, however, are only shallowly researched, especially those that provide information about a lot of family members. It is worth remembering the following statistical information about family histories: there is a positive correlation between the number of individuals covered and the degree of boringness. The more individuals a family history documents, the more tedious it will be to read. So, to write a gripping family history, we must ask ourselves how many family members we are willing to research in exhaustive detail and focus solely on those. The output of our indepth research will be a series of *biographies*.

In *Writing Interesting Family Histories*, I discuss different ways in which we can structure a family history – that is, ways we can group these biographies – so I won't elaborate any further here.

2. History

Our ancestors didn't drift through space. Their feet walked firmly along history's highways. Each of our ancestors was, in his or her own way, an embodiment of the times. Yet many family historians fail to include any information about the historical context, except to mention a date and a place in passing. Not only does this omission prevent them from doing justice to their ancestors' lives, they miss an ideal opportunity to add life to their narrative.

If there is nothing in our ancestor's life that, on the surface, will help us write a gripping biography, then the historical backdrop is of particular importance.

The reference to 'history' in the family history three-legged stool refers to everything associated with our family's backdrop. To write *Chubbie Miller*, I had to research aviation in general, the Golden Age of Aviation (1927-1932), female aviators in general, specific aviators like Amelia Earhart and Bert Hinkler (who were friends and rivals of my protagonist, Jessie 'Chubbie' Miller), aircraft manufacturing companies and their planes, the countries and towns Chubbie travelled to, and the political, social and economic factors that impacted her story.

Here is an example of how we can use background information to increase the drama of our stories. For a number of months, Chubbie flew a revolutionary plane called the Eaglerock Bullet. In December 1930, she disappeared while flying over the Florida Strait. While researching her story, I discovered that the Eaglerock Bullet had been nicknamed the 'Killer Bullet' or the 'jinxed' plane. Needing more detailed information, I purchased via Amazon.com a privately-published book about the Eaglerock planes, a book that wasn't available in any Australian library.

Using information from the book, I was able to generate a sense of foreboding that commenced long before readers reached the chapters covering her disappearance. I did so by describing some of the plane's problems, as shown below:

> Chubbie knew the risks [of accepting a job as a test pilot]. Indeed, what pilot hadn't heard the stories about the Alexander Aircraft

Company's problems with its revolutionary Eaglerock Bullet? ... For commercial sales, the plane needed to pass stringent government accreditation tests including those that changed the plane's centre of gravity by moving crates of sand loaded on board. The Bullet's first accreditation test pilot ... successfully parachuted out when he encountered a deadly problem and was paid $100 for his endeavours. A week later, the widow of the second was paid $250. The third demanded $500 to put the plane through the rigorous certification process. He too had a successful bail out. The fourth demanded $1000 in advance before he flew the plane, and the money passed to his estate.

Researching the background history is – and should be – as much fun as researching our biographical subjects. We never know what information we will stumble across that might help us bring an ancestor's biography to life. While researching *Chubbie Miller*, I also discovered that my male protagonist had a friend named Mervyn Rylance who had once been the business partner of the infamous murderer, Dr Crippin. Frustratingly, I had to cut out the paragraph because my manuscript was too long. For someone else, though, that single piece of information could help transform a dry biography into something intriguing.

If we make sure that we fully flesh-out the lives of EACH of our biographical subjects and write gripping prose, when we combine the biographies together we will have a gripping family history.

To most family historians who read Charles Rich's full internet biography, it would seem as if there was little that could be used to produce gripping narrative. In fact, if we look closely we can glimpse something. The author mentions in passing that Charles was the chaplain at the Cockatoo Island penal settlement. Surprisingly, the author fails to mention that Charles was later the chaplain at Darlinghurst Gaol. The gaol saw at least one execution a year during Charles' service there. As chaplain, Charles attended to the doomed convicts in the weeks before their execution, was responsible for telling them that the execution would go ahead when their appeals failed, listened to their final prayers and confessions, walked before them to the gallows reciting the service for the burial of the dead, and stood beside the gallows watching as they fell to their deaths. Some of these executions are graphically described by the press, particularly those that went disastrously wrong – like that of my black widow, Louisa Collins. Many of these executions were also socially controversial and politically divisive.

Once we think about how Charles' life intersected with the lives of the convicts on Cockatoo Island and in Darlinghurst Gaol, we can envisage how his life story could be set against the backdrop of crime and criminality in the 1800s, or of penal servitude and the continued use of capital punishment, or of the bushranging epidemic of the 1860s. By making these themes part of the narrative arc (see chapter six), we can transform his life story into a gripping biography. And we can offer insights and enlightenment about Charles himself and his times. If we offer personal and historical insights and enlightenment, we take our family histories to a level rarely found in the genealogical world.

In the following paragraphs, which are extracted from *Black Widow*, the information comes from Charles' reports to the press and we see the scene through his own eyes:

> Canon Rich's hopes of a reprieve hadn't been realised. He had stayed with Louisa until late the previous evening, praying with her and offering every ounce of spiritual comfort he could summon. He had joined her on her walk to the condemned cell, where they knelt together and continued their prayers. There had been no word from the governor. Louisa was going to hang.
>
> He tentatively broached the subject of a confession. She sidestepped his urgings by claiming to have confessed all her sins to Almighty God and to have begged for his forgiveness.
>
> Was this a tacit admission? He had long realised that she of all people was unlikely to confess to a mere mortal. A confession to God was probably all that could be hoped for …

Charles is also mentioned in the dramatic description of Louisa's ghastly execution. In *Black Widow*, we watch her execution through the journalists' eyes; however, a family historian attempting to write gripping narrative would describe the scene through Charles' eyes. Writing 'point of view' in discussed in chapter five.

Each of my mainstream books tells the tale of an individual (or pair or group of individuals) whose life was more remarkable than those of most of our ancestors. I stumbled across three of these stories while researching one of my ancestral lines, and I mentioned the stories in the resulting family history. Descendants of some of these people and their associates are alive today. Interestingly, most knew nothing about their ancestors' dramatic lives or their ancestors' involvement in dramatic stories (as employers, employees, friends, witnesses) until they began researching their family histories. Thus, some people's family histories *do* include gripping stories. As often as not, though, the seeds of a gripping biography will be found only when we conduct broader background research.

Let me make you a promise. There is always something interesting out there. My writing career is founded upon it. And in the following pages I will provide strategies to help you find that 'something' to bring life to your own family history.

3. Story

Telling a biography as a story is the best way to transform dry facts into gripping narrative. I will cover this component in less detail here, though, because it is the subject of the next six chapters.

Suffice it to say that a good story – in the true sense of the word *story* – has five distinct stages: an originating event, rising action, climax, falling action and resolution. We can follow this structure when we craft the tale of an incident in our ancestors' lives. We can also follow it when we craft their life stories in their entirety.

To make these stories gripping, we need to weave in action, drama and sensory description. Overall, we need to ensure that we communicate a sense of tension. A story without tension is just a chronology: this happened then this happened then this happened. Family histories are, of course, mostly chronologies. Add tension, though, and our readers will be hooked.

3

Visualising facts

How do we find the stories – or, at least, the facts and background history that we can turn into stories – that will transform our dull biographies into gripping narratives?

The first thing we have to do is to change our mental focus when we think about the information we have gathered for our ancestors. Most family historians perceive their ancestors' lives as a list of facts rather than as a series of events. For example, when I previously discussed Reverend Charles Rich's internet biography, I observed that his biographer failed to mention the blindingly obvious: that the references to Charles' directory listings were in fact references to Charles' residence.

So where do we find the 'event' in those directory listings? Let's start with the visual.

The visualisation process

Every directory listing describes a three-dimensional dwelling in a three-dimensional street. It might be a single house, a semi-detached, a terrace or apartments. The block of land might have a large front garden containing brightly-colour flowers or a small courtyard with a few potted plants or a front door that opened directly onto the street. The dwelling might be in an upmarket district among other expensive properties, or in a middle-of-the-road suburb, or in a run-down area. The street might have nearby shops or be a purely residential location. It might be busy and noisy with through-traffic or be a quiet cul-de-sac.

This means that each directory listing describes something that our ancestors could see. So let's picture this scene as a photographic image. We've all looked at old black-and-white photographs so we shouldn't find it too hard. Some of us will have already gone to our ancestor's street address and seen the house itself so it will be easier to picture the area. Some will have seen a picture of the house or street. Others will now think, 'Hmmm … must add "go to street and find house" or "look in picture libraries" to my task list.'

Next, let's picture this scene as a video. We see people gardening or walking along the street or standing in groups chatting. We hear children squealing, dogs barking, vehicles honking. We smell the bouquet of fresh flowers and the stink of dunny cans.

Then we ask ourselves: which of the above most accurately depicts Charles' world? The sentence 'He was listed in a directory dated …'? Or the black-and-white photograph? Or the colour video?

The answer is simple. The video. Most black-and-white facts in documentary records represent three-dimensional scenes that are full of colour, action and life.

That being the case, how do we transform 'He was listed in a directory' into a video? The answer is also simple. We use our imagination.

Imagination

When I mention imagination to non-fiction writers, I often see their eyes widen. Indeed, a look of horror crosses some faces. This is because they define imagination as something that produces:

> … a conception or mental creation,
> often a baseless or fanciful one.

That is, they see *imagination* as the vehicle used to create works of fiction, the antithesis of works of non-fiction. But note: this definition of imagination is the fourth in the list of Dictionary.com definitions. The first-listed definition is:

> The faculty of imagining,
> or forming mental images or concepts
> of what is not actually present to the senses.

Read this definition a couple of times because it is extremely important. While certain images and concepts may not be *present* today, in terms of being mentioned in surviving documentary records relating to our individual ancestors, they were certainly present in our ancestors' lives. And through exhaustive research into the world of yesteryear, we can use our prose to make them present again in our family histories.

Thus, if we can take this definition of imagination on board, we have begun our journey to writing gripping biographies.

Using our imagination

When we read the directory entry that lists Rev Charles Rich as residing at 140 Waterloo Street, Sydney, we don't just picture a page with words on it. We imagine what is not actually present on the page. We imagine the scene the directory entry represents.

And when we eyeball another directory and read that Charles resided at 147 Dowling Street, we remember that every change in directory listing reflects a change in residence. But we don't just picture another street scene. We picture a residential relocation. Packing boxes. Furniture removalists – presumably horse-drawn in those days. We remind ourselves that, for our ancestor, reality is not the directory listing but the experience of living in one house, packing, moving to another house, unpacking, and living in the new house. And we remember that some people hate moving house because they find residential relocations emotionally traumatic as well as expensive. In the dry wit of Benjamin Franklin:

> Three moves are as bad as one fire.

Event versus documentation of event

One of the problems with most family histories is that they refer to the documentation of the event rather than the event itself.

Let's think about a piece of information every genealogist has to deal with: a person's birth. Everyone who is writing a family history has been born and has also given birth or had a partner who has given birth or knows someone who has given birth. We have seen images of women giving birth in pictures, photographs, movies and documentaries. We know what happens and we know how dramatic it can be.

I have two children and each birth was dramatic. We lived a 50-minute freeway drive from the hospital when my first child was born but had been told that it wouldn't be a problem because labour begins slowly with contractions every 25 or 30 minutes. We planned to drive to my parents as soon as I went into labour and then drive the few minutes from there to the hospital when it was time. Instead, I went straight into fast hard labour. We had to crawl along the freeway at 4 am in a torrential rainstorm while I had contractions every five minutes. Do I remember the event in dramatic detail? Oh yes! Is it a story I tell? Yes.

Every mother who reads this anecdote will now be thinking about her own children's births and how dramatic and life-changing they were. No doubt every mother has told the tale of each of her children's births at least once, if not many times. Yet how many mothers have told the tale of filling out or providing information for their child's birth certificate. Indeed, how many mothers would even remember when they prepared it or what they wrote on it?

Despite the fact that our own memories are of the birth event itself, when we don our family historian hats we usually limit our account to the mere mention of the birth's occurrence and documentation. Using the Sarah Adams' example from *Writing Interesting Family Histories*, most family historians write:

> Sarah Adams was born on 1 February 1799 in Deal, Kent, England ....

What did the church record list?

> Sarah Adams   Born 1 February 1799   Deal   ...

Is there any reference in this type of prose to the physical acts of conception, pregnancy and delivery? No.

The odds, of course, are that we know nothing about our ancestor's birth and probably have no interest in crafting a story about any birth or births. The point of this example is to show – using an event that everyone can relate to – how family historians focus on the documentation of an event and ignore the event itself.

That's why it is so important to visualise an event and see if it tells a story we can use for our family history.

For the sake of argument, what if we wanted to write something interesting about a woman for whom little is known other than that she was a mother? Is there anything we can draw upon?

Think about the feelings of a woman who kept losing her babies during or shortly after childbirth? Think not only about her grief but her feeling of being a failure. When a woman's primary role was to bear children, those who couldn't successfully do so were pitied and looked down upon.

We talked in the previous chapter about context. Think about the time of year. Did the birth occur in the depths of winter or perhaps in the heat of summer? Was a trained midwife in attendance or was the mother cared for by a family member? Was she living in a city, where she might have recourse to a doctor or hospital in the event of trouble, or in an urban setting?

A friend's ancestor fell off a horse and died on the same day his wife had a baby. Perhaps he was on the way to get a midwife or doctor. Or perhaps he celebrated the birth too much and lost control of the horse on his way home. Behind those two dates lies a story.

Story boards and videos

If a timeline for our biographical subject is already prepared, look at the entries and imagine them as a series of story-board images, the type that film directors use to visually display their stories prior to filming. If an entry looks like it has story-telling potential, imagine it as a YouTube video.

When we encounter a baptism timeline entry, instead of picturing a church register with black ink on a white page, imagine a scene with parents standing near the font in a packed church. We see them hand their baby to the clergyman, who dips his hand into the water and sprinkles it onto the infant's forehead. We hear the infant's scream at the touch of the cold water.

When we read a census entry, instead of seeing a page listing family groups with their pertinent details, imagine a census collector trudging along the street, knocking at our ancestor's door, asking for the head of the house, writing down the details he provides, and so on.

It is only when we begin to think about each fact as an event, and each event as a potential story, that we step further along the pathway to writing gripping biographies.

Events and stories

Is there an event of some sort in every timeline entry? Yes. Absolutely. Someone had to do something physical to produce the information found in the entry, if only to copy information from one book to another.

Is each event a story? No. There is no story, for example, in the act of a clerk copying information from one book to another – unless the story lies in our frustration that he made an error.

One thing we can know for certain, though, is that the greater the number of entries listed in our timeline, the more likely we are to find some good stories. And the only way we can generate long timelines is if we conduct exhaustive research.

Here is an easy way to find good stories. Look at the timeline and ask which entries reflect events that our ancestor would have remembered for a long time? Which events are most likely to have generated a tale that our ancestor told in later years?

Birthing stories, of course, are among them. Migrant stories are as well. Imagine the stories our ancestors could tell if they had left their families in the United Kingdom and emigrated to another country. Most people living in Australia, New Zealand, America, Canada and South Africa will have at least one migrant ancestor.

And what about death stories? We find a will made by our ancestor signed in shaky handwriting three weeks before his death. There's a story in that. The ingredients are: an ill husband and father; a doctor telling him that it's time to get his affairs in order (as suggested by the details on his death certificate); and his acceptance that this needs to be done to help and protect the family.

Other stories will be unique to our own family histories. These include the examples mentioned in the next chapter.

4

Telling a story

Imagine we are writing our memoir. Would we write the following about our first day at school?

> I started school on 3 February 1960 when I was five years old. I left home at 8.22 am and walked 456 yards, arriving there at 8.43. The bell rang at 8.55 and we went into the classroom. It was 30 feet by 28 feet with a 12-foot high ceiling. There were 36 other children in the room. The bell rang for recess at 10.50 and ...

Of course we wouldn't. We would talk about our feelings and emotions and about the teachers and other pupils and what we did in the classroom and in the playground. Yet what is listed above – the dry emotionless facts – is effectively what most of us write in our family histories:

> Sarah Adams was born in Deal, Kent, England on 1 February 1799 to John Adams, a blacksmith, and his wife Mary, nee Jones. She was baptised on 24 March 1799 at St Mary's Church of England, Deal ...

Most family historians seem content to write a tedious account of their ancestor's life even though they know, on some level, that they would never write their own memoir in such a way.

Of course, the argument from family historians is that they want to stick with the facts, that they want to communicate only what they know. But how many of us would want to read a biography of Marilyn Monroe or Napoleon that stuck only to the facts? Very few, I suspect. We would be bored in a few pages – as most people are with family histories. The most interesting biographies are written by authors who allow themselves to read between the lines and make judgements, who offer insights and enlightenment. They use other strategies as well that are discussed in the following pages.

Minimise and maximise

The best non-fiction writers employ the tools of fiction-writing rather than encyclopaedic- or academic-writing to assist with the development of their story.

Because my current book, *Chubbie Miller*, is an action-packed tale of adventure, drama, mystery and tragedy, I purchased lots of Kindle books on fiction-writing to help develop my dramatic-writing skills. Every book offered something new. One of the lessons that particularly resonated with me was the following:

> Write slow scenes fast and fast scenes slow.

Essentially, this means that we should skim over the 'boring' facts by describing them briefly and that we should focus most of our energy and words on the drama-filled scenes. So let's rephrase it so we can easily remember it:

> Keep dry facts to a minimum and expand drama to the maximum.

I once read a family history (which was of a better standard than most) in which the author reduced one of the most dramatic events in the family's life to two brief sentences. Intruders had attempted to enter the family's bedroom one night but were deterred when the father grabbed his shotgun. Imagine how frightening it must have been for the family. Imagine how often they would have told the tale of the night they were nearly murdered in their beds (yes, they would have embroidered the tale until it barely resembled the truth!). Yet the author described the scene in only 30 words at the end of a paragraph. It would have barely blipped on a reader's radar.

On the previous page of that same family history, the author devoted three paragraphs to the background history of the area – dryly factual information that took the reader back as far as pre-European settlement. And on the same page as the intruder tale, the author spent a few paragraphs describing the construction of the property, change of ownership, repairs, layout and so on. The author mentioned the area's isolation and the presence of ruffians and bushrangers before referring to the intruder incident but treated these ominous portents as if they were of no more interest than the description of the property's construction and repairs

This family historian managed to transform a potentially dramatic and gripping scene into one that slipped past almost unnoticed because she focused her attention on the dry facts and skimmed over the drama.

A practical example

In my own writing, I had already grasped the idea of telling dramatic scenes as if they were occurring in slow motion. Yet reading the 'write slow scenes fast …' advice helped me to fully understand what I was trying to achieve and to do a better job of it.

The best way to explain this principle is to provide an example. In *Chubbie Miller*, my protagonist was a passenger on a flight from England to Australia. The plane had two separate open cockpits, with Chubbie sitting in the front and Bill, the pilot, in the back. They communicated by shouting over the engine noise or by sending messages through an open hatchway under Chubbie's seat. They had a dramatic landing in Rangoon just before Christmas 1927 and were forced to remain there – penniless – until the New Year.

First of all, I needed to communicate a sense of their location but didn't want to devote too many words to the dry facts hence the following short paragraph of three sentences:

> Meanwhile, at least sightseeing was free. Burma was still loosely under the control of the British Raj. When they stood in some parts of the city looking at its neat colonial buildings and churches and ornamental gardens, it was easy to imagine they were standing in any British city – until they glimpsed the longyi-dressed locals and the Shwedagon Pagoda, with its gigantic golden stupa rising towards the heavens.

Just as an aside, this is an example of description seen through the eyes of the protagonist. As discussed in *Writing Interesting Family Histories*, descriptions like these move the story along because they are part of the protagonist's experiences rather than being a block of add-on text that the reader skips.

The drama-filled incident that followed was allowed considerably more words. A brief description of the incident and some sentences of dialogue were included in contemporary newspaper reports, Chubbie's post-flight account and her later interviews. Using this information as a foundation, I expanded the scene and slowed it down to make the most of the drama:

Early Monday morning, they set off from Rangoon to head across the Gulf of Martaban before continuing south down Burma's narrow coastal territory. About twenty minutes into their journey, the plane started to lurch up and down like a bucking bronco. It dived suddenly, but pulled up again a moment later. Then it bounded around as if Bill had lost all control of the joystick.

Chubbie turned in her seat and shrieked, 'What's the matter?'

Bill shouted back a single, unexpected, terrifying word: 'Snake!'

The plane had been moving swiftly when he spotted the brown snake uncurling itself from under Chubbie's seat. About three feet in length, it had a flat head attached to a dark cylindrical body with a blunt tail. He had no idea what type of snake it was or whether it was dangerous or not. He wasn't going to wait around to find out.

Unable to leave the controls to deal with the emergency, his only choice was to take his feet off the rudder and try to stamp on it – hence the strange lurches and bounds as he attempted to maintain control of the plane. The last thing he needed was to be fighting a stalled engine, a diving plane and a potentially deadly snake at the same time.

When he failed to crush the snake, the wily creature slithered through the open hatchway under Chubbie's seat. 'Look out!' he screamed to Chubbie, and pointed towards the floor.

*

Just before they left Rangoon, Chubbie's hostess had said to her, 'Do not forget! Before you leave, have a good look in the machine for snakes. Your machine has been out in the field for some time, and all those swamps are infested with snakes. You might find that you are carrying an extra passenger if you do not make a search.'

Chubbie had thought the woman was pulling her leg. She was so relieved that the engine was repaired and the plane was out of the paddy field and they had cash warming their pockets, that the warning slipped from her mind. Until now.

Seeing Bill pointing towards the ground, she looked down at her own cockpit floor. She saw an inquisitive head peeping up at her from her side of the hatchway.

Never before had she removed her joystick from its clip so quickly. She whipped it into the air and whacked the snake over and over again. Blood spurted everywhere. She opened her eyes – half-closed in horror during her murderous rampage – and looked more closely. It didn't move. It looked dead. She waited for a moment longer. When it still didn't move, she reached down and picked up its bloodied body and tossed it over the side of the plane.

Later they learnt that the snake was called a krait and was one of the deadliest in the India/Burma region …

Now, I could have told this dramatic tale in a single paragraph by writing:

Shortly after they left Rangoon, Bill saw a three-foot long snake in his cockpit. He tried to stomp on it but it slid into Chubbie's cockpit. She bludgeoned it to death with her joystick and threw it over the side of the plane.

Which is the more gripping?

Differences between the two versions

The most obvious difference between the above two descriptions is the word length. The longer description is nearly 500 words. The shorter description is less than 50. However, there are a number of other significant differences.

In writing the long description, I employed the ideas that came to me during my clothes-line epiphany. I wrote the long version in the 'active voice narrative' whereas the short description is the usual 'passive voice narrative'; that is, I allowed the characters to act out the incident rather than intruding as a narrator to tell the reader what happened. I described the incident by telling the tale as a 'story'; story-telling is discussed further in next few chapters. And I followed the writers' mantra 'show don't tell'.

Showing and telling

What do I mean by 'show don't tell'? In the long version, I *show* the reader what is happening by allowing Chubbie and Bill to *act out* their own story. We, the reader, feel as if we are in their cockpits, if not inside their heads – note in the long version I stated, '*Chubbie had **thought** the woman was pulling her leg*' – and we are living the experience with them.

In the short version, I *tell* the reader what happened. It is merely a *recount* of the facts. It is how most family historians communicate the details of their ancestors' lives – even the dramatic incidents.

The phrase 'show don't tell' is found in most writing books and is one that every writer should memorise. I'll repeat it again.

Show don't tell!

When we scan our timelines looking for entries that might be transformed into a story, make a point of pausing at any that reflect some sort of physical action. If appears appropriate, let our biographical subjects act out the scene and milk it for every bit of drama we can extract.

Action scenes are the best fun to write. In fact, when I begin writing one of my books, I usually begin with an action scene.

Summary

Keep dry facts to a minimum and expand drama to the maximum.

5

Point of View

All prose reflects a perspective. All prose is communicated through someone's eyes.

This might seem to state the blindingly obvious because all prose is written by an author so of course it communicates what the author sees. However, there is a difference between *authorial voice* and *narrative voice*. Each work of prose contains a narrative voice (or voices) that is deliberately – or perhaps unwittingly – chosen by the author as the vehicle of communication.

Let's start by talking about 'person' in the grammatical sense.

Person

Remember when we were at school, we were taught about writing prose in the 'first person' – that is, with 'I' or 'we' as the subject. Or the second person – 'you'. Or the third person – 'he', 'she', 'they'. While some novels are written in the first person, most non-fiction books, except memoirs, are written in the third person.

It is essential that we stick to our 'person' when writing prose. Here is a problem example taken from a lengthy LinkedIn biography:

> Working with us will provide you the knowledge of who you are through discovering those who have gone before you … David loves what he does and does it well. He customizes his research to give you what you want, whether it is a record of the steps he took … We can provide what you want …

The author referred to himself as 'us' then as 'David' (fake name) then as 'we'. So, not only does he jump from the first person to the third person and back again, he jumps from the plural to the singular and back again.

This biographical piece was probably a cut-and-paste job without an edit. Nonetheless, for someone who is attempting to sell his professional services, it comes across as unprofessional because of the 'person' confusion.

When we write in the first person, our readers feel as if they are inside the heads of our protagonists seeing the world through their eyes. When we write in the third person, our readers feel as if they are standing in the distance watching the protagonists. The difference is referred to as *immediacy*. First person writing is more *immediate* than third person writing because we feel closer to the protagonist of our story.

As family historians, we are most likely to be writing in the third person so we'll focus hereafter on the third person point of view.

Headspace

The two snake-in-the-plane versions reflect different points of view. When we read the longer version, we see that it starts from the perspective of what is called the *omniscient narrator*, the all-seeing eye. The omniscient narrator is positioned outside the plane – effectively – and describes what it sees and knows:

> Early Monday morning, they set off from Rangoon to head across the Gulf of Martaban before continuing south down Burma's narrow coastal territory ...

For anyone struggling with the concept of an omniscient narrator, imagine that this narrator is sitting in a neighbouring plane with a video camera and is filming what is happening to Chubbie and Bill and their plane.

After the word 'Snake!', the camera zooms in so far it slips inside Bill's head. We see what he is seeing and hear his thoughts:

> The plane had been moving swiftly when he spotted the brown snake uncurling itself from under Chubbie's seat ... He had no idea what type of snake it was ...

In the last sentence before the dinkus (the asterisk between the two sections), Bill mentions Chubbie. This acts like a baton changeover in a relay race. It allows the camera to comfortably leave Bill's head and slip inside Chubbie's head without the reader feeling confused about the change in point of view. From then on, we hear Chubbie's thoughts and see her actions as if we are looking at the scene through her eyes.

> 'Look out!' he screamed to Chubbie, and pointed towards the floor.
>
> *
>
> Just before they left Rangoon, Chubbie's hostess had said to her, 'Do not forget! Before you leave, have a good look in the machine for snakes …'
>
> Chubbie had thought the woman was pulling her leg. She was so relieved that the engine was repaired and the plane was out of the paddy field and they had cash warming their pockets, that the warning had slipped from her mind. Until now …

As an aside, the extract above doesn't need the dinkus to communicate that a change in point of view is coming. Bill's cry to Chubbie to 'Look out!' is suggestive enough. Instead, the dinkus tells us that a bigger change than viewpoint alone is about to occur. In this instance, it allows us to jump into Chubbie's head and to communicate a *flashback*, which takes us back to Rangoon.

Read the entire long version again to see the different points of view in action.

The short snake-in-the-plane version reflects only one point of view, that of the omniscient narrator. This all-seeing eye not only sees the scene from a distance, it can see into Bill and Chubbie's separate cockpits:

> Shortly after they left Rangoon, Bill saw a three-foot long snake in his cockpit. He tried to stomp on it but it slid into Chubbie's cockpit. She bludgeoned it to death with her joystick ….

The omniscient narrator point of view is the easiest to write; however, it inevitably creates a sense of distance between the protagonist and the reader. Only an extremely skilled writer can overcome this problem and generate gripping prose.

Headspace switches

It is essential that we don't switch points of view midstream. Here is an example of a problematic paragraph from the author of a self-published book about Thunderbolt:

> He broke the spell with a reassuring grin [to Mary Ann], and then urged his mount through the fog ahead. That native beauty that, thunder-and-lightening-like, claimed his attention sixteen years ago struck him anew. She was gazing at the love of her life, and the dying moments of that love. She had more than an inkling that all she treasured was about to be taken from her ...

The author starts the paragraph by allowing us to hear Thunderbolt's thoughts; that is, the author is telling his tale through Thunderbolt's point of view. In the third sentence, however, the author jumps into Mary Ann's head and we hear her thoughts, her point of view. The switch mid-paragraph is bizarre and disorienting. It is also bad writing. It would never survive a professional edit.

Viewpoint switches – or at least switches between biographical subjects – are common mid-paragraph in family histories although they are not normally as obvious because the writing style is more distant. In the edit phase of any writing, it is helpful to make sure that the subject of our paragraph remains the same throughout the paragraph. If we have started a paragraph by writing about the husband then switched to writing about the wife in the same paragraph, we should consider inserting a paragraph break between the two references. If so, we will probably have to tweak the phrasing to ensure a natural flow between the two paragraphs.

In the short version of the snake-in-the-plane incident, it might appear at first glance that there is a subject switch from Bill to Chubbie. In this instance, though, the subject of the paragraph is in fact the snake.

Omniscient versus close third

One of the reasons subject switches are not as obvious in family histories is because there are different ways of writing in the third person. Most family histories and other works of non-fiction are written from the omniscient narrator point of view. Most fiction – these days, at least – is written from the viewpoint known as *close third* or *limited third*. I prefer the phrase *close third* because it is easier to visualise and therefore to teach.

So what is the difference between the omniscient narrator and the close third points of view? In the headspace section, I talked first about the camera being outside the plane, saying that this represents the omniscient narrator viewpoint. When the camera moves inside Bill's head, it represents the close third viewpoint. Close third creates greater immediacy for readers because it makes them feel as if they are seeing the world through the protagonist's eyes.

To show the difference, I have extracted examples from a first draft version and the published version of *Black Widow*. Let's start with the first draft version, which is told from the viewpoint of the omniscient narrator:

> Hugh Hart Lusk was asked by Justice Foster if he would defend Louisa Collins in her murder trial, which was scheduled to begin the following week. The judge said that there wasn't any money to pay for his services.

Do you feel a sense of distance between yourself and the two characters as if the scene is being narrated by an outsider? That feeling of distance is one of the signs that prose is written from the omniscient narrator point of view.

Now let's examine the published version, which reflects the close third point of view:

> One week, that's all he had, one week to prepare a defence in a murder trial. The prosecution had had a month. And they'd had the government's coffers to draw upon, and the witnesses' depositions to peruse. What did he have? A request from Justice Foster that he, Hugh Hart Lusk, should conduct the case *pro bono*, which meant no fee, no assistance, no money for any investigative work and a huge tranche out of his income-generating hours.

When we read the second version, we feel as if we are in Hugh Lusk's head as he thinks about his options in a panicky way.

So, why do we feel as if we are in Lusk's head? It's really simple. It begins with the use of pronouns.

Pronouns

Many writers – including international bestselling authors – seem to think that the protagonist's name and the relevant pronoun are interchangeable. They seem to think that, if they have used the pronoun a few times, they should mention the subject's name again for a bit of variety then the pronoun and then the name again and so on.

WRONG!

I have written 'wrong' in capital letters to make it clear that this view is erroneous, untrue, false, inaccurate, incorrect, unsound, mistaken and completely misguided.

My unwitting discovery of the most effective way to use pronouns is one of the reasons I keep getting book contracts. Seriously.

Let's examine the differences. The first version commences with Lusk's full name: 'Hugh Hart Lusk was asked …'. This makes us feel as if we are being *told* what is happening by someone who is watching the scene.

The second version, however, uses the pronoun 'he' in the first sentence: 'One week, that's all he had …' This produces an intimate feeling as if we are closer to the protagonist (and it sparks curiousity in the reader as we wonder who 'he' is). Soon the phraseology generates an edgy feel as if we are hearing the protagonist's panicking thoughts. His full name isn't introduced until sentence five and, when it is introduced, it seems like he is calling *himself* 'Hugh Hart Lusk' so we continue to feel as if we are hearing him think.

I have used these two variations of the same Lusk information to show the power of a pronoun in generating a sense of intimacy and immediacy for the reader.

At some point, usually at the start of a book or chapter or section, we have no choice but to identify for the reader the person whose point of view they are about to hear. We do so (usually) by giving them a name. When we call them by that name it almost always creates a moment of distance.

To generate a close-third immediacy, the trick is to call the protagonist *he* or *she* as much as we can. When we identify the person by name, we can do so unobtrusively, as I did with the second Lusk example or, more often than not, we boldly call them by their name at the start in order to identify them and to get the momentary sense of distance over and done with. Thereafter we use the relevant pronoun for as long as possible. For pages and pages if possible. The result, if the rest of the prose is also suitably intimate, is engrossing.

Failure to properly use the *Charles* and *he* options was among the many problems with Rich's prose timeline on page 13. Sentences one, three, six, seven and eight called him *he* while sentences four and five called him *Charles*. Given the context – a bald recitation of the facts – sentence one should have identified him as *Charles* and all later sentences should have referred to him as *he*.

There is a problem with learning how to use the name/pronoun combination properly, though. It can reduce our reading pleasure. Once we become comfortable writing in this way, we soon notice when other authors fail to maintain the 'in the head' pronoun and keep dragging us out of the narrative by their use of the protagonist's first name or surname. It becomes really irritating – enough, I have found, for me to give up on authors who should know how to best use pronouns. It's not rocket science. Some books on writing mention the technique so I'm not the only writer to work it out.

Generating close third

Writing in the close third point of view doesn't only require a change in pronoun, of course. We need to feel as if we are in the head of our protagonist and are seeing the world through his or her eyes. This is extremely difficult for many family historians to write, particularly those who have previously focused only on writing prose timelines. It requires a mental gear shift.

Here is a trick to help with that gear shift. I haven't used it myself because it only occurred to me recently when I was thinking about techniques to help family history writing students. If only I had thought of it earlier. In the past, I had to resort to a couple of stiff drinks to get in the zone. Now it comes naturally.

Imagine you are your ancestor and you're experiencing the incident you want to write about. Now write the description in the *first person*, that is, 'I was … I did … I saw …' Polish the prose until it is intimate and gripping. Then change the pronouns from the first person to the *third person*; that is, 'I' to 'he' or 'she'.

If you've included thoughts and feelings in the first person version, these can be trickier to change. However, with really intimate close third, we can communicate our own perception of what our ancestor would be thinking or feeling without specifically stating that he or she is thinking or feeling it. This is what I did with the close third paragraph about Hugh Lusk. We hear his 'thoughts', or what seem to be his thoughts, and we feel as if he is overwhelmed and panicky without it specifically being stated.

The close third viewpoint allows us to *show* the reader what is happening whereas when we use the omniscient narrator viewpoint we tend to *tell* the reader what is happening. Thus, the *active voice narrative*, the *close third* point of view, the ability to *show* rather than *tell*, and the focus on *story-telling* are all interwoven aspects of gripping writing.

Choosing point of view

When we write a family history in which we devote a chapter to a person, it is obvious who our biographical subject is. We may use our prose to communicate their point of view. Or we may use the omniscient narrator perspective to communicate our own view of their world. Whether we intend to or not, we are always communicating someone's perspective.

In my books, I move from omniscient narrator to close third and back again depending on what I am trying to communicate and how I am attempting to do so. The long version of the snake-in-the-plane incident showed the movement from omniscient narrator in the first paragraph to close third in the middle paragraphs, and then back again to omniscient narrator in the last sentence.

I recently grasped, after reading Marcy Kennedy's *Point of View in Fiction*, that the main reason why I sometimes struggled for hours to get going, writing-wise, was because I was struggling to work out whose point of view to use. In *Chubbie Miller*, for instance, my primary protagonist is Chubbie; however Bill, her flying partner, is almost as important. As often as possible, I wanted to communicate Chubbie's viewpoint although I sometimes needed to tackle the subject from Bill's point of view and required a natural way of handing over the baton. On other occasions, I wanted to communicate whatever was happening from the viewpoint of a bystander. Understanding that my struggle was caused by this viewpoint problem proved a major breakthrough in my writing. Gone are the days when I wasted hours of writing time.

This might be a breakthrough for others who are writing from a perspective other than that of the omniscient narrator. If so, I recommend Marcy Kennedy's book (see the Reading List).

Given name versus surname

The more 'up close and personal' we are in our writing style, the easier our books are to read. That being the case, another way we can make our readers feel closer to our biographical subject is to use his or her first name rather than surname. I recently read a David Baldacci book in which all of the characters – including the women – were called by their surnames. The characters themselves called each other by their given names, but the author called them by their surnames. It had a surprisingly distancing effect, particularly when used for the women.

For our family history purposes, we don't want to create any more distance than we need to.

One argument for using a person's surname rather than given name is that there were so many people in the past with the same given names. However, we should have clearly identified the subject of our biography – for example, 'John Stanley Smith' – at the beginning of his biography so if we refer to 'John' elsewhere in his biography the reader will assume – quite rightly – that we are referring to our biographical subject.

In my mainstream books, I tend to refer to my main characters by their given names. The unimportant characters are referred to by their given name/surname combinations or as *Brown* for a man and *Mrs Brown* for a woman, or whatever else is relevant. This is probably a useful system for family historians and overcomes the problem of common given names.

Full name versus given name

I once read a family history in which the author used the character's full name, including middle names, every time she mentioned the person, with only the occasional use of pronouns. Prose-wise, the effect was heavy and cumbersome. Reading-wise, it was exhausting. The argument was that other members of the family had the same given name and surname so the full name was necessary to distinguish one person from another.

But here's the thing. As mentioned above, once we have clearly identified our biographical subject, there is no need to keep telling our readers his or her name. We should provide the person's full name when we first introduce him or her then use pronouns thereafter where possible. We call our subject by name again – almost always using the given name only – if we have mentioned someone else and need to refocus the readers' attention on our subject. If we mention someone else with the same name, it is better if we identify that person by their relationship to our subject.

For example, if we are writing a biography about John Stanley Smith and we have occasion to refer to his son, who was also called John, it is better to say that 'he received a visit from his son John' rather than that 'he received a visit from John Thomas Smith' or '… from his son John Thomas Smith.' Think readable rather than pedantic. No doubt we will have noted somewhere else, perhaps in a reference to John's children's births, that the child was named 'John Thomas' so there is no need to repeat the full name.

Summary

Point of view is something most writers and readers never think about. Yet, similarly to the Supreme Court Justice in the landmark pornography case who famously said, 'I know it when I see it', we are all intrinsically aware of 'point of view' and we notice it when the author messes it up.

6

Direction

My husband and I go to the movies every week and recently saw *The Lady in the Van* with the esteemed Maggie Smith. To say that this film has a slow beginning is an understatement. My husband fell into a doze. I would have switched it off if I had been watching Netflix. It turned out to be a good movie so it was fortunate we were forced to keep watching. But, as someone who is constantly thinking of ways to improve my own writing and to help family history students, it led me to ponder why it was so boring. I realised that there were two reasons: lack of direction and lack of tension. These are discussed in this chapter and the next.

Direction or through-line

When a family historian writes, say, a surname-line family history, it is clear to the reader where the book is heading. It is even clearer if the author includes a brief structural description in the introduction or author's note, and a family tree chart to visually communicate the structure (discussed further in *Writing Interesting Family Histories.*)

In writer-speak, this structure provides the family history's through-line. A *through-line* is, according to Dictionary.com, 'a theme or idea that runs from the beginning to the end of a book'. In a family history, the through-line is usually the family's surname. When we pick up a book titled *The History of the Forman Family of Stirling, Stirlingshire, Scotland*, we have a pretty good idea of what the book is about, what the through-line is.

In the chapters within a family history, the through-line should also be obvious. So, for example, in a *pole-shaped* family history – that is, one that follows our ancestral line for a single surname down as many generations as we have found – the through-line reflects the different generations in a natural chronological sequence. Generation one is our first-known ancestor with that surname, say, Patrick Forman (1692-1750). Generation two is his son, John Forman (1720-1756). Generation three is his grandson, Thomas Forman (1746-1800), and so on. If, however, we inserted a biography about James Smith (1920-1950) between generations two and three, we would leave the reader feeling completely confused because we have broken the through-line. The surname is different and the timeframe is different. This is an example of a 'dog's dinner' mentioned in *Writing Interesting Family Histories*.

So what was the directional or through-line problem with *The Lady in the Van*? Viewers had no idea where the story was heading, no sense of a through-line. To summarise: an old lady was living in a van parked on a well-to-do street. The local residents weren't happy but no one did anything about it. Moreover, there was no sign that anyone *was* intending to do anything about it. So there was no sense of the direction the story was to take. All we knew, for quite some time, was that there was a crotchety old lady living in a van parked on the street. No wonder my husband fell asleep.

Digressions

Not only is it important that our story has a clear through-line, it is critical that we stick to that through-line, not necessarily rigidly but at least loosely. Digressions should only be included if they tie in somehow with the through-line. After detailing the digression, the author needs to quickly and smoothly return to the through-line so the reader doesn't start to feel lost. That being the case, it is critical that we don't include compounding digressions in our family histories.

Let me explain by way of an example. My first venture into writing popular history, *An Irresistible Temptation*, tells the story of a sex scandal in the late 1820s in colonial New South Wales, which contributed to Britain's decision to recall the controversial governor. The two protagonists were Jane New and John Stephen Jr. When I introduced John, I talked about his family background.

John happened to be the grandson of James Stephen, a friend of William Wilberforce. James and his namesake son, John's uncle, were prominent members of William Wilberforce's anti-slavery group, one that was pivotal in legislating to abolish Britain's slave trade. Including this information was a digression from the main story line however it was a relevant digression. The abolition of slavery was driven by social progressives, and the Stephen family in New South Wales were prominent progressives who locked horns with the conservative New South Wales governor. Thus, progressive versus conservative politics was an important theme of the story.

John's father was sent out to Australia to sit on the New South Wales Supreme Court and John joined the family there a few years later. In writing about John's father, I talked about his voyage to Australia and included a few paragraphs about an incident on board the ship in which the ship's captain sold his daughter to another ship's captain. It was a great story but it was a double digression. Not only was John Sr's voyage to Australia irrelevant to the progressive versus conservative theme, the selling of the captain's daughter was even more irrelevant. I ended up cutting this section of the story from the manuscript because it deviated too far from the through-line.

Let's think about digressions from a family history perspective. Perhaps we mention in our family history that a neighbour acted as the midwife at our ancestor's birth. We mention that the neighbour had originally come from Germany. Then we mention that, during the neighbour's journey, the ship's captain sold his daughter to another sea captain. Again, this is a double digression and a completely irrelevant one. If we include that sort of digression in our family history, our readers will scratch their heads and say 'What … ? Why are you telling me this? How does this fit into the story?'

Genealogists have a tendency to throw everything they find into a family history whether it is relevant or not. I once saw a draft family history that included a page of information about a man for whom I could see no obvious connection to the family being written about. I asked the author what the person's connection was. The author struggled to remember. It turned out that the person had some distant connection to the family and that the author had found the information and had added it to the family history. But he had failed to mention the connection so it looked like a page floating in limbo. As it happened, the information was uninteresting and irrelevant, just stuff he had found. It was better deleted not only because it was a digression but because it was boring.

Remember this: all digressions must progress our story in one way or another. If they don't, be ruthless. Delete them.

Narrative Arc

While the through-line communicates the overarching theme, the *narrative arc* represents the development of the unfolding biography.

Most family histories don't have a narrative arc other than the chronological because they don't tell a story – not in the real sense of a story, that is (narrative arcs and story-telling are discussed further in the next chapter). Most family histories are merely a series of chapters covering different members of the family, with each chapter documenting a simple chronology: birth ... marriage ... death. These types of family histories are the easiest to write because the structure is so obvious to the writer and the reader.

If we want to make them more interesting, we have to work within the chapters themselves to communicate a *theme* or through-line other than the merely chronological (see 'thematic structures' below). This isn't as hard as it might seem because most biographical-style narratives follow a loosely chronological structure that progresses forwards through time. Sometimes, though, they contain *flashbacks* (which are discussed further in the next chapter).

For example, *The Peculiar Case of the Electric Constable* tells the story of the first murderer apprehended by means of the electric telegraph and the consequences kick-started the Communication Revolution. Section one tells the story in the *present* – that is, the dramatic events of New Year's Day 1845 – whereas section two is a flashback that tells how the protagonist found himself in the situation that ended section one. From section three onwards, the story progresses chronologically.

This strategy meant that readers became invested in the story and in the protagonist himself and were willing to bear with me when I narrated what were, initially at least, the less dramatic facts of his back-story (birth, residence, etc.). This strategy can also be used to create reader tension, which is discussed in the next chapter.

Thematic structures

All books have themes of one sort or another. As mentioned above, the main theme of most family histories is the chronological account of the relevant family's actions and movements. Any other subject is generally mentioned only in passing.

Similarly to most family histories, my mainstream books have a loosely chronological through-line that helps move the story forward. However, each book also contains a series of themes.

For example, *Breaking the Bank* tells the story of a group of convicts in the penal settlement of New South Wales who tunnelled through a sewerage drain and stole the equivalent of $20,000 in today's terms. One of the themes of the story is the upstairs/ downstairs politics of colonial New South Wales. The broader community of serving and emancipated convicts (the 'downstairs' in the social community) refused to tell the authorities (the 'upstairs') the names of those who had committed the crime or who had passed stolen money to them even though they faced harsh punishments for their intransigence. Thus, the book doesn't merely recount what happened; it offers insight and enlightenment into a certain period in colonial Australian history.

My fifth book, *Black Widow*, tells the story of Australia's first female serial killer and has as its themes the growing movements in favour of women's rights and against capital punishment. Again, Louisa's story is set against this backdrop and offers insights and … Are you getting the message?

Did I know that these would be important themes when I decided to write these stories? Definitely not. I stumbled across these social issues while conducting my research. They piqued my curiosity so I explored the subjects in depth and wove the issues through the stories.

A family history will be much more interesting for our readers if we use it to communicate more than just the usual who-begat-whom, if we use it to communicate a bigger picture theme. What could that be?

If we have migrants in our ancestry, the 'push' and 'pull' factors are an obvious theme, the factors that pushed them out of their homeland and that pulled them towards the country they eventually settled in. Indeed, any social or political or economic issue of the time could be used as a theme. Obviously, we need to read history books to know what was happening during the period covered by our family histories. Online newspapers – or the much harder to access microfilms – are even better if we are interested in a narrow timeframe. Our ancestors' lives might be a reflection of the times or alternatively, if our ancestor was a Luddite for example, they might show a resistance to the times. This brings us back to the three-legged stool discussed in chapter two. To write gripping biographies, it is essential that we explore the historical backdrop.

The theme or themes we discover can become secondary through-lines that carry the story forward. Most will be relevant only to a single individual or a single generation. Some might run through the entire family history. Whatever we find, whatever we use, we can be certain of one thing: ANY theme is more interesting than just the simple hatches/matches/dispatches chronology followed in chapter after chapter after endless chapter of the average family history.

So try to think if there is anything historical or social or even technological that could add life and depth to a family history. It's there, I promise. Look for it. Find it. Use it.

7

Story development

Our brains love stories. Since pre-historic times, humans have used stories to communicate social, moral and political messages. Religions are the longest-lasting examples of these story-telling traditions.

Most people think of a story as something that has a beginning, middle and ending. That's true. However, the Greek philosopher, Aristotle, advised that while a story does indeed have these three parts, the beginning is not simply the first incident in a three-part chronology. Rather, it is an originating event that engages the reader. The middle follows on naturally but, importantly, it is not simply pieces of random information lumped together (as most family histories are). The information in this section needs to be causally related to the originating event. And the ending is the inevitable conclusive event.

For this reason, most family histories are not *stories* as such. They are merely a series of biographies that are themselves chronologies. At best, we find the occasional story told within the various chronologies.

It is extremely difficult even for an experienced author to write a multi-generational family history as a *story*. That being the case, my focus in the following chapters is on individual biographies as potential stories, as well as incidents within those biographies.

Story structure
It is more helpful for learner story-writers to divide stories into five parts: originating event, rising action, climax, falling action, conclusive event or resolution. These parts are discussed below and are best communicated using examples.

1. Originating event

Most family history biographies don't have an originating event. They start with 'Sarah Adams was born on …'

In *Chubbie Miller*, the originating event for the entire book was the arrival of Charles Lindbergh in London after his record-setting flight from New York to Paris in May 1927. This forms the prologue and introduces Chubbie, who was holidaying in London at the time.

Chubbie's *back-story*, which provides her birth details, doesn't commence until a few paragraphs into chapter one. This is to ensure that the reader is engaged enough with her character to be willing to read the dry bits. The facts of the first twenty-five years of her life are zipped through in three or four pages of the 350-ish page book because we must 'keep dry facts to a minimum'. This gets us back to the timeframe of the originating event – in writing terms *the present* – and the story progresses from there as if it is happening in the here-and-now.

Just as an aside, writing in *the present* does not mean writing in the *present tense*. It means writing in the past tense as if the incident has just happened, which is how the long snake-in-the-plane incident is written.

Most family histories don't have a present, a here-and-now. The entire publication is crafted as if an omniscient narrator is recounting what happened a long time ago.

In the snake-in-the-plane scene, the originating event was the snake's decision to sleep in the plane. If this incident was written as a simple chronology, the snake's presence in the plane would be mentioned at the start. But that would be boring. Gripping prose leaves the reader wondering what is happening for as long as possible. The information is gradually revealed as an unfolding mystery (which is discussed further in chapter eight).

What could serve as the originating event in a family history? For migrant ancestors, an obvious originating event – an event that could act as a prologue – is the moment they stand at the dock looking at their ship of departure. Behind them is everything they have known, everyone they have known. In front of them is the exciting yet terrifying unknown. Once they step on that ship, there is no turning back. Thus, even if we knew nothing other than the fact that our ancestor left Liverpool, England on 12 June 1842 on the *Eugenia*, we could craft a dramatic biographical beginning using sensory description alone (covered in chapters nine to fifteen).

If this incident becomes our originating event, we can communicate our ancestor's story as if it is happening in the present. This generates a sense of immediacy, as if the reader is living the experience with them. If we know very little about the events leading up to our ancestor's decision to migrate, we can communicate the past as a *back-story*. If we have more information, and want to communicate that information as if it were also being experienced in the present, we communicate it as a *flashback*.

Before we move on the step two, let's look at back-stories and flashbacks by way of examples.

Back-story

When we communicate a back-story, we jump from the present to the past and communicate what happened in the past as if it were in the past. In *Chubbie Miller*, I introduced Chubbie in the prologue (the present) and began chapter one as if it were still the present and we are hearing Chubbie talk to us. The end of this present section is shown in the first paragraph below. The dinkus (the asterisk) indicates a change in perspective. In this instance, the change is from Chubbie's point-of-view to that of the omniscient narrator. It also indicates a time-frame change. In the post-dinkus paragraph, the omniscient narrator recounts what happened during the previous twenty-five years of Chubbie's life.

> [London] couldn't have been more different to the constrained and insular world she had come from, the world that was dragging her back as each day of her six-month holiday ticked away.
>
> *
>
> She was born Jessie Maude Beveridge on 13 September 1901 in what, by comparison, was the middle of nowhere: the town of Southern Cross sitting on Western Australia's flat red earth, 230 miles from Perth at the western terminus of a railway line ...

Flashback

A flashback is different. Below is another example from *Peculiar Case*. In the top paragraph, the story is told in the present from the police's point of view. After the dinkus, it jumps to the apothecary's viewpoint and communicates what happened a few days previously as if it were also happening in the present. This means that we are not forced to tell a story as a strictly chronological account. It allows us to have a big *reveal*. And when we do reveal all, we still have the immediacy and tension of the present. We continue to *show* the reader what was happening by allowing the characters to live their own stories rather than *telling* them what happened in the past.

> Commissioner Rowan had leaflets printed. He ordered the beat constables to leave them at the apothecary shops they visited … Then Police Constable Edmund White called at an apothecary situated at 89 Bishopsgate Street, just a few minutes' walk from Cornwall.
>
> *
>
> Manager Henry Thomas had been working at the counter of Surgeon Hughes' apothecary on the previous Wednesday when a man dressed in Quaker garb and a greatcoat walked in. Thomas recognised him. He was a regular customer …
>
> 'Can I have two drachms of Scheele's prussic acid?' the Quaker asked, pulling from his pocket a small half-ounce phial. He handed it over and said that it could be used to fill the order.

2. Rising action

Family histories rarely have any rising action. They are usually a plod from one fact-filled recitation to another. Even a potentially dramatic incident is usually told as a chronological recount rather than as a story.

In the snake-in-the-plane incident, the rising action was Bill and Chubbie's attempts to kill the wily snake.

What makes rising action gripping is when it involves *complications*. Books on thriller-writing suggest compounding the tension by adding complication after complication as did the Greek tragedians and the great Bard himself.

In the snake-in-the-plane incident, the obvious complications are the snake's potential deadliness, their airborne status, and Chubbie's inability to land a plane. The unspoken complications include the inhospitable terrain beneath them and the lack of medical services.

In a migrant experience in which the originating event has our ancestor standing at the dock looking at the ship of departure, we could skim through the birth-details and other dry facts as a back-story. When we reach the point where our ancestor is starting to think about migrating, we commence the scene as if it were happening in the present. This allows us to develop the story – the rising action component – as our ancestor considers the options.

You might be thinking at this point, 'But I know nothing about what they were thinking?' In fact, you do. We all do. Every one of us has had to make a major change-of-life decision at some point. And, as is explained in chapter fifteen, not only do we all experience a range of emotions at any given time, our total number of emotion groups is surprisingly small. In a situation like this, our ancestors would logically be considering the advantages or disadvantages. They would be thinking, 'Should I or shouldn't I?' They would make a tentative decision then second-guess themselves. How do I know? Because they are human. Have you ever made a major life-changing decision without second-guessing yourself?

Attempting to communicate what our ancestors would have felt at important moments of their lives moves beyond the dry facts to the essence of their lives. This is probably a good point to repeat the words of Hannah Farnham Lee (also included in *Writing Interesting Family Histories*):

> A mere compilation of facts presents only the skeleton of History; we do but little for her if we cannot invest her with life, clothe her in the habiliments of her day, and enable her to call forth the sympathies of succeeding generations.

We can only draw forth 'the sympathies of succeeding generations' if we can communicate some sense of our ancestors' emotions. This is discussed further in chapter fifteen.

3. Climax

Family histories rarely have any climaxes. They usually plod from birth through marriage to death, with no change of pace or sense of developing tension.

In the snake-in-the plane incident, the climax was the moment Chubbie killed the snake.

In a migrant experience, the climax depends on how much happens in our ancestors' lives. The climax to one migrant story might be the moment our ancestor steps onto the ship's deck and accepts that there is no return. The journey itself might represent the *falling* action and resolution, the pause before another story begins, the story of their arrival in the New World.

Of course, the moment of embarkation might not have been the climax to their story. What if a spouse or child died during the voyage?

Whatever the migration story, it was a life-changing experience for our ancestors. And each migrant's experience was different, to some extent. Some migrants, such as those travelling from Europe to America, fully intended to return to their homeland. Italians had their 'birds of passage' for whom migration was a money-making exercise; they passed back and forth repeatedly between Italy and America. For most Irish, the departure was permanent and was imbued with little nostalgia or doubt but rather a 'good riddance' relief, given the destitute conditions they had left and the promise that awaited them. And Nazism forced many to leave their European homelands forever.

Considering how important the migration experience was to our ancestors, we must attempt to fully understand it and communicate it to our readers in such a way that we 'call forth the sympathies of succeeding generations'.

4. Falling action

Without a climax there can, of course, be no sense of the action falling away, of the pace slowing towards an incident's resolution.

In the snake-in-the plane incident, the falling action is Chubbie's recognition that she has killed the snake and her decision to toss its carcase overboard.

5. Conclusive event or resolution

The resolution in the snake-in-the-plane incident is our – and their – realisation that if Chubbie hadn't killed the snake it would probably have killed them.

Stories within stories

Have you ever played with a Russian Matryoshka Doll? A friend had one when I was a child and it was fun opening the outside doll and finding another identical but smaller doll inside then opening the smaller doll and finding another one inside until we eventually reached the tiny doll in the centre.

That's what a good book is like. It is layers of stories within stories. Again, let me explain by way of an example.

As mentioned above, the originating event in *Chubbie Miller* was Lindbergh's arrival in England which is covered in the prologue. Chapter one introduces Chubbie. Chapter two introduces Bill. The rest of section one tells the tale of their drama-filled flight to Australia. It contains a series of stories like the snake-in-the-plane incident. Each of these stories follows the five-part story-telling structure discussed in this chapter (originating event, rising action, climax, falling action, resolution).

The flight itself – that is, most of section one – also follows the same five-part structure, with one of the dramatic stories near the end of the section (not the snake-in-the-plane incident) serving as the section climax.

The book is composed of four different sections. Each section contains a series of stories, and each of those stories joins together to create the larger story at the heart of the relevant section, with a climax near the end.

Finally, each of those four sections comes together to create the *Chubbie Miller* book in its entirety, which has its own five-part story structure and its final climax in the epilogue.

Our lives are also a series of stories. Some occurred while we were at school, which are stories within the bigger story of our school-life. Some occurred while we were employed doing a certain job. These are stories within the bigger story of that particular job, which is a story within the bigger story of our working career. And so on.

Of course, most events in our lives do not form stories in the true sense of a *story*. They could be better described as *scenes* and *sequels* as discussed below.

Scene and sequel

I once saw a movie that was non-stop action for the entire ninety minutes. What was worse was that its backing music was loud and intense. There was no let-up in the action or the music's intensity. By the time the movie finished, I felt like I had gone through a wringer.

The problem was that this movie had no *pace* or *rhythm*. It sat in the same gear throughout: overdrive.

If we take a car trip, we travel along flat stretches then up hills and down valleys and along more flat stretches before we reach another hill. The hills are like the drama-filled *stories* in our life history, the stories that rise to a climax and fall away again. Let's call these the *scenes*, as they do in the movies. The flat stretches are the boring everyday parts of our lives, the natural interludes between the *scenes*. These are the *sequels*.

A well-written biography is composed of a series of scene-sequel sequences. We maximise the drama-filled scenes and keep the detail in the sequels to a minimum.

Thus, when we look through our timelines, we are not only seeking stories or scenes. We need information that precedes or follows the scenes to help give our prose pace and rhythm. We don't need to include everything we have found because, if we have prepared a timeline for our biographical subject, the information is accessible through the timeline. What we need is something that keeps the readers' attention and that appropriately carries us to the next scene. This allows our prose to flow smoothly from one story to another. It also allows each biography to flow seamlessly from the start to the finish.

And, if we think about the big picture, each biography within our family history should also form part of a scene-sequel sequence.

The first biography serves as the scene. We then include something that connects the two biographies – something other than the obvious father-son relationship (or whatever) – so that the second biography follows on smoothly from the first. And so on.

A family history that is merely a series of consecutive biographies will otherwise seem jerky in flow and formulaic in nature.

Summary
To write family histories that grip our readers, we must all take off our genealogist hats and become story-tellers.

8

Tension

Travel writers have long realised that the best holidays are those in which nothing goes wrong yet the best holiday stories are the ones where everything goes wrong.

All good writing is travel writing, in one form or another. This is because the protagonist takes a metaphorical journey – for example, from ignorance to enlightenment. The best stories are those in which the protagonist encounters obstacles along the way. In fact, as most books on writing reveal, a story isn't a *story* unless something goes wrong.

Fiction-writing books refer to the something-going-wrong issue as *conflict*. As a non-fiction writer, I prefer to describe it as *tension*.

When I ask family history writing students to offer suggestions as to why novels are much easier to read than encyclopaedia articles, they offer many suggestions: story-telling, description, sensory information, dialogue, layout, and so on. *Tension* or *conflict* is never mentioned. Yet it is an essential component of any good novel.

Back to the *Lady in the Van*. If there had been any suggestion that the locals were going to take action to get rid of her and her van, legally or otherwise, the story would not only have had a direction, it would have had some dramatic tension. Without tension, it doesn't matter how descriptive, conversational or visually dynamic a book is, readers will soon get bored.

I have never read a family history that contained even a hint of tension. Mine didn't. Yet somehow, while writing that first popular history – probably in the moment I discovered story-telling – I realised that I needed to use the type of tension-generating strategies I had noticed in thrillers and crime-fiction.

Tension is found in tales of drama, mystery, tragedy and romance.

My latest book has all of these ingredients so I've had to work out strategies for dealing with them. Let's discuss romance first.

Romance

It is extremely difficult to communicate romance effectively in a non-fiction book. I can't. In fact, I doubt if anyone but an extremely skilled fiction-writer could do so. We can allude to it – the marriage offer and acceptance, the meeting with the clergyman, the posting of marriage banns and the attendance at necessary services. We could even perhaps offer a look between the engaged pair denoting 'This is real!' But don't try to get down to the nitty gritty. It will come across as twee if not cringe-worthy and embarrassing.

Tragedy

Tragedy can also be difficult to communicate effectively. First, it is important to remember that every death is not a 'tragedy'. Dictionary.com defines *tragedy* as:

> A lamentable, dreadful, or fatal event or affair; calamity; disaster.

That being the case, the deaths of the elderly are not 'tragic' whereas the deaths of those on board the *Titanic* were 'tragic'.

If we *tell* our readers what happened in our ancestor's life, if a death was indeed tragic, we are forced to *tell* the reader so. However, if we *show* the reader what happened by allowing the story to unfold in the present (as discussed in the previous chapter), the tragic nature of the event speaks for itself.

Drama

We can find sources of drama anywhere in our family histories. An approaching birth or death or journey. A conflict between family members. The second half of this chapter includes a number of strategies to help us add drama and tension to our family histories.

Mystery

As we write our family histories, we tend to forget that we know what happened in our ancestors' lives – in the big picture at least – but they didn't. The future was always a mystery to them.

One way to communicate a sense of that mystery is to write their stories in the present as if our ancestors are living their own stories rather than history-watchers recounting it for them. The very fact that 'what happens next' is unknown to them – and therefore to our readers – is an immediate source of mystery and tension, if we use our writing skills to communicate it effectively.

Another mystery-generating strategy is to reveal information gradually rather than dumping it all on the reader at the start. Robin Annear's *The Man Who Lost Himself* is a wonderful telling of the Tichborne claimant story, the legal cause célèbre of Victorian England. Thomas Castro, a butcher from Wagga Wagga, Australia, claimed to be the missing Tichborne heir. In Annear's book, the mystery unfolds in such a way that one moment the reader thinks that Castro was indeed Roger Tichborne and the next 'of course he wasn't', then the reader jumps back to 'maybe he was' and so on. We can do the same, on a smaller scale, in our own family histories.

Tension-generating techniques are discussed below.

Cutaway

One way we can generate tension is by using the filming technique known as the *cutaway*. We reach a certain point in our tale then 'cut away' to introduce something or someone else, leaving the reader hanging. In the long snake-in-the-plane incident, the dinkus served as the cutaway, as shown below:

> When he failed to crush the snake, the wily creature slithered through the open hatchway under Chubbie's seat. 'Look out!' he screamed to Chubbie, and pointed towards the floor.
>
> *
>
> Just before they left Rangoon, Chubbie's hostess had said to her, 'Do not forget! Before you leave …

In this example, the cutaway leaves our readers on their edge of seats, knowing that the snake is heading into Chubbie's tiny cockpit, while we cut away to a time before the plane departed. The trick with a cutaway is to slow down the pace, to expand the description, to drag out the backstory – or whatever else we have cut away to – until readers are desperate to know what is happening back at the cliff-hanging moment. Then we return to the drama at hand.

Ticking clock

To anyone today who reads a novel about the *Titanic*, it is a 'ticking clock' tale. We know what happened. We long to warn those on board the ship, as they party the night away, that they are sailing towards disaster. But we can't. And every so often, the author ramps up the tension by mentioning the time. Tick … tick …

A woman waiting for her baby's birth is a potential ticking clock tale – even if nothing bad ends up happening. Remember: the bomb under the café table, the bomb that readers know about but the coffee drinkers don't, doesn't always go off.

When we seek stories in our timelines, we are looking for anything that has the potential to communicate tension. Then we use whatever strategies are at hand for communicating that tension.

Hooks

'Last night I dreamt …'

Most female readers of my own or my parents' generation can finish the above sentence. It is the first line in Daphne DuMaurier's best-selling novel *Rebecca* and states in full, 'Last night I dreamt I was at Mandalay again.' I don't know why it is such a memorable line but it is.

As mentioned in section two, 95% of unsolicited manuscripts are dismissed by publishers even before they reach the bottom of the first page. The author has failed to *hook* the publisher's interest. I discuss hooks in *Writing Interesting Family Histories* but have added further information below.

Here are a few suggestions for hooking our reader's interest at the start of our family histories.

1. Intrigue our readers. Make them wonder.

Simon Winchester started the preface to *The Surgeon of Crowthorne* with:

Popular myth has it that one of the most remarkable conversations in modern literary history took place on a cool and misty late autumn afternoon in 1896, in the small village of Crowthorne in Berkshire.

This intriguing first sentence piques our curiosity in so many ways. We want to know what was said in that conversation and why whatever was said was remarkable, indeed, why it was so remarkable that it gave rise to a popular (that is, well-known or famous) myth. We want to know who participated in the conversation, how it impacted modern literary history, and what was relevant about the year, season, time of day, weather and location.

2. Begin at a pivotal point in our story.
Winchester's preface recounts the tale of the meeting between his two protagonists. They had regularly corresponded for twenty years but one of the protagonists had no idea who the other really was. That awakening of knowledge occurs at this meeting. Then the first chapter begins with a critical moment in the back-story, which is told in. Gradually, the back-story to this back-story unfolds. Clever writing.

3. Create an evocative picture.
Daniel James Brown in *The Boys in the Boat* (another great book) commences his prologue with the following:

> This book was born on a cold, drizzly, late spring day when I clambered over the split-rail cedar fence that surrounds my pasture and made my way through wet woods to the modest frame house where Joe Rantz lay dying.

Of course, this is also a pivotal moment in the writing of the story because it is a description of a journey of discovery. These are discussed in more detail in *Writing Interesting Family Histories*.

Foreshadowing
We can use foreshadowing to create tension, as shown below. My protagonist Chubbie Miller flew in the first ever women's air

race (nicknamed the Powder Puff Derby) and I ended a chapter as follows:

> Some of the derbyists had already had an hour or two of sleep, others none at all. They would get little more because of their early wake-up call. Logan's intransigence meant that these female pilots, who hadn't experienced the military training given to most of the world's elite male pilots, would have to fly over rugged mountain ranges and hot desert floors while suffering from sleep deprivation. It was a recipe for trouble if ever there was one.

Of course, our foreshadowing might be a red herring. In fact, it is a good idea to have some red herrings in the pie to keep our readers guessing. In this case, it wasn't a red herring.

Epigraphs

Epigraphs are the quotes at the start of a chapter under the chapter number or title. Family history writers can use them to add tension or drama or mystery to their publication.

In the first two editions of *Writing Interesting Family Histories*, I wrote a couple of pages about epigraphs. In the latest edition, I have devoted an entire chapter to the subject. That being the case, I will say nothing further here except to provide an example of a tension-inducing epigraph:

> Oh, well, it's a good way in which to commit suicide.
>
> Aviator Sir Keith Smith to
> Captain William Newton Lancaster and Chubbie Miller, 1927

9

Sensory writing

Our world is a world of the senses. Think about the impact on our lives if we lost the ability to see or hear or smell or taste or touch.

In *Writing Interesting Family Histories*, I discussed the importance of communicating the reality of our ancestors' experiences by providing sensory descriptions rather than simply documenting the facts. Sensory description is a critical component of any gripping story so it is covered in the next series of chapters.

As mentioned previously, most family histories are prose timelines with chunks of description scattered between the timeline entries. Think about a family history that documents a migrant ancestor. The usual style is to list the date when the ancestor left England – or wherever – and the name of the ship of departure. This is the prose timeline component. Then comes the chunk of description, which is often included in a separate paragraph. If it describes the ship itself, it might report that the ship was a sixty-foot, four-masted schooner that was built in Calcutta in 1790 and had an A1 rating from Lloyds. Then comes another paragraph of prose-timeline information reporting that our ancestors reached a certain port of call on a certain date. Then comes another chunk of description. It might describe the country or the port/town itself and could mention facts like the date of European settlement, the population breakdown, the size of the country or town, the terrain and so on.

What these writers forget is that much of this information would be unknown to our ancestors and, moreover, would be of little interest to them. Would they have cared when or where their ship was built? If we are going to include this type of factual information, we need to say why it might have been relevant to our ancestors' lives. For example, if the ship was built in 1790 and had an A1 Lloyd's rating, and if our ancestor travelled on the ship in 1795, this information suggests that the ship was seaworthy and was likely to carry them safely to their destination.

As an aside, a reference to the fact that a ship was *likely* to carry them safely to their new country generates a sense of foreboding (if written well) because it raises the possibility that this subject is being introduced to presage the fact that the ship *doesn't* transport them safely. This generates tension which, as discussed in the last chapter, is a primary ingredient in gripping writing.

What mattered most to our ancestors were not the dry facts of the journey but their sensory experiences. Think about what they would have seen and heard and smelt and emotionally felt when they reached their port of embarkation and saw their ship of emigration. Think about their sensory experiences as they embarked, sailed from port, crossed the ocean and stopped at a port of call or at their final destination. Think about what they would have seen and heard and smelt and emotionally felt when they looked from the deck towards the town or port of their new homeland.

When family historians include sensory descriptions, they usually stick to the visual. However, our ancestors experienced the world through all of their senses, as we do. So let's explore ways in which we can add life to our family histories by including sensory descriptions. In the following pages a chapter is devoted to each of our senses.

An extremely helpful book that discusses sensory descriptions is Rayne Hall's *Writing Vivid Descriptions*, which costs only a few dollars on Kindle.

10

Sight

'In Victorian England,' writes Simon Winchester in his wonderful book, *The Surgeon of Crowthorne* (aka *The Professor and the Madman*),

> even in a place as louche and notoriously crime-ridden as the Lambeth Marsh, the sound of gun-shots was a rare event indeed. The Marsh was a sinister place, a jumble of slums and sin that crouched, dark and ogre-like, on the bank of the Thames just across from Westminster …

What a sinister impression this master of non-fiction has communicated in only a few words.

There are many ways we can communicate evocative descriptions that primarily draw on the visual. These are discussed below.

Descriptions of people

Since we are writing family histories, it is probably best to first talk about descriptions of people. Some family historians provide physical descriptions of their ancestors, drawing the information from paintings or photographs.

Of course, most of us have no images of ancestors who died before the mid-late 1800s. However, information can be found in other sources. Military records, for example, contain detailed physical descriptions so that pen portraits could be published in the event of a desertion. When John Williams deserted from Lewes Barracks in England in 1806, the *Hue and Cry* described him as being 5'8" with a fair-ruddy complexion, hazel-grey eyes, and sandy or red hair and eyebrows (probably 'strawberry blonde' in today's terminology). He had an oval-shaped head, thin face, long nose and small mouth.

He also had a long neck, square shoulders, long arms, thick hands, a thin build, thin legs and small feet. What a description.

Conversely, his companion-in-desertion was the same height but was as broad as Williams was thin. They must have looked like a nineteenth-century version of Laurel and Hardy. No wonder they were recaptured.

Most visual descriptions in family histories stick to the facts. They refer to a person's hair colour, eye colour, nose size and complexion along with their height and build. However, descriptions that include authorial judgements are much more interesting. Peter Cochrane wrote about the British Prime Minister, Earl Grey:

> He was a knobbly gangling fellow, all joints and limbs in that thin tube of a frock-coat and tall topper, a stick insect of a man with the face of a frog.

The best physical or character descriptions require the authors to go beyond the literal to the metaphorical as we can see in Cochrane's description of Earl Grey as being a 'stick insect of a man with the face of a frog'.

Simon Winchester focused on character and intelligence more than physical appearance when he captured a person's essence in the following:

> A total clown, an ass, a scandalous dandy, and a fool.

Saying the same thing in different ways can be powerful and unforgettable, but don't overuse it as a writing strategy.

Winchester also used movement to communicate character and personality attributes in the following description:

> … a policeman, plodding and imperturbable.

Descriptions of faces

When I was researching *Black Widow*, I discovered that a physiognomist had written a monograph about Louisa Collins. Physiognomy was a pseudo-science that was fashionable in the 1800s. It was founded on the belief that we can judge character by facial and skull characteristics. So I googled 'physiognomy facial features personality' and came up with ideas I could draw on in my word portrait of her. It turns out that we still use many of its ideas in our assessments of individuals – or perhaps its ideas came from common beliefs.

I already had the basics for Louisa – hair-colour, eye-colour and so on – from her prison records and trial reports. But I wanted to communicate character as much as the physical facts. And I didn't want the details to be dumped into the narrative like the chunks of description discussed in the previous chapter. Instead, I wanted them to come out naturally as the story unfolded. So I wrote:

> Marshall frowned at the woman in confusion. Her plea suggested that her husband was a patient and had received recent medical treatment, yet the man's name sparked no memories. Nor was the woman herself familiar – a handsome woman, he observed, with heavy-lidded brown eyes and a sensual face framed by dark hair, although long past the bloom of youth.

This description *showed* Marshall seeing her. Conversely, Cochrane and Winchester's descriptions involved the author *telling* the reader what their subjects looked like – with exquisite prose.

Recently I discovered an extremely useful source of descriptive information: *How to Write Descriptions of Eyes and Faces* by Val Kovalin, which costs only a few dollars on Kindle.

Our faces are made up of many different components, any of which could be drawn upon for our pen portraits. Below are some suggestions to trigger thoughts. We can use a thesaurus, such as the online Thesaurus.com, to come up with more variations.

Don't just think about the words themselves, think about what they represent. A round face, for example, might seem exotic. Or it might seem moon-like and suggestive of stupidity. A heart-shaped face might seem pretty, although perhaps too pretty for a man.

Face
Shape: round, oval, heart, square, diamond.
Width: wide, broad, chubby, plump, pudgy, fat, narrow, thin.

Height: long, short. A long narrow face can seem horse-like.
Colour: fresh, peaches-and-cream, olive, red (choleric), ruddy.
Hardness: angular, blunt, craggy, lined, rugged, sculptured.
Softness: delicate, ethereal, fine-boned,.
Texture: fine, thick, coarse, silky, velvety.
Blemishedness: freckled, pimply, pock-marked, scarred.
Hairiness: bearded, bristly, stubbled.
Impression: careworn, gaunt, haggard, tired, wizened.

Hair

Colour: blonde, flaxen, auburn, red, ebony, raven, grey, white.
Texture: coarse, thin, fine, thick, sleek.
Waviness: straight, wavy, curly, frizzy.
Other: bald, balding, patchy.

Ears

Size: great, big, large, small, delicate.
Projectingness: elephantine, goofy.
Shape: pointy, square, round.
Lobe shape: long, attached, fleshy.

Forehead

Tallness: can suggest intelligence but too high seems eggheaded.
Shortness: can suggest lack of intelligence, thick, dull-witted.
Creasedness: furrowed, anxious, brooding.
Uncreasedness: unfurrowed, calm, confident, immature, shallow.

Eyebrows

Shape &c.: thin, thick, arched, straight, hairy, wispy.

Eyes

Colour: black, brown, hazel, amber, green, blue, grey, violet.
Shape: protruding, fish-like, heavy-lidded, slanty, cat-like.

Nose

Shape: see below; also bulbous, pinched, snub.

Long & straight: called a 'Greek' nose from statues.
Convex: aquiline, beaky, a 'Roman' nose, a proboscis, honker.
Long & slightly convex: elegant, regal.
Short & convex: fierce, falcon-like.
Impression: aristocratic, disdainful, cheeky.

Cheekbones
Shape: high (can be delicate, pretty), broad (exotic).

Lips
Shape: thin, pinched, thick, fleshy, bow-shaped.
Colour. red, crimson, pink, purple, blue, washed out.

Chin
Shape &c.: sharp, pointed, square, bristly.
Impression: blunt, stubborn, determined, weak.

Neck
Shape: long, swan-like, short, squat, bull-like, jowly.

Physique
Width: broad, chubby, plump, fat, slender, scrawny, waif-like.
Appearance (animal-like): beefy, bovine, brutish, reptilian.

Judgement
Positive: beautiful, pretty, handsome.
Middling: homely, plain, ordinary.
Negative: ugly, gross.
Temperament/countenance: angelic, cherubic, devilish, impish.

A man could have an aquiline nose *sculptured* like a Roman god's or a woman could have skin that was *silkily smooth*.

It isn't necessary, of course, to use all of these groups in our descriptions of a person – indeed, it is highly advisable not to. The point is to allow us to see physical attributes we might not have noticed without these trigger words. And once we have a list of literal words to describe a person's physical appearance, we can think about branching out into the metaphorical.

Description of places, objects &c.

Simon Winchester also mixed the literal with the metaphorical when he referred to Lambeth Marsh as a 'jumble of slums and sin'.

When we *see* something in the world around us, there are many layers to what we are seeing, many more than most of us realise. Again, we need to burrow down to find the individual ingredients.

Size

Height: huge, big, middling, small, tiny, minuscule.

Width: thin, narrow, fat, wide, broad and so on.

Bulk: heavy, dense, light, fluffy, wispy.

From there we can branch out to more descriptive words and phrases. We could say that something was so small it was *Lilliputian-like* or so large and bulky it was like a *colossus*. We could expand the visual to include a sense of movement and power when we say that something was like a *relentless juggernaut*.

Shape

Roundness: circular, conical, oval, round, spherical.

Squareness: cubic, rectangular, right-angled.

Straightness: flat, perpendicular, horizontal, vertical.

Curviness: curling, meandering, sinuous, snaking, winding.

Levelness &c: flat, sloping, steep, undulating.

Sharpness &c: jagged, pointy, razor-like, spiky, blunt, dull.

Swollenness: bulbous (nose), bulging (eyes), bloated (face).

Impression: squat, hunkering.

We could mention a *conical* mountain, a *sinuous* river, a *pointy* roof. We could refer to a *wisp* of smoke *curling* from a *squat* chimney.

Texture

Smoothness: clean, even, neat, silky, unblemished, varnished.

Unevenness: bubbly, carved, embossed, grainy, imprinted.

Roughness: abrasive, coarse, gnarled, gravelly.

Pattern

When we focus on patterns, we tend to think about clothes: checked, spotted, striped and so on. But think about patterns in the landscape; for example, the *checkerboard* or *mosaic* pattern of agricultural fields. And think about farm-houses *dotting* the landscape and roads *criss-crossing* the countryside. The words *dotting* and *criss-crossing* are verbs so they also add strength to our writing.

Colours

There are many ways to describe colours. Google 'words for colours' and it pulls up some useful lists. Colour words include:

Colour variations: blue, aquamarine, cobalt, indigo, navy.
Colour adjectives: ashen, bleached, rich, sheer, streaked.
Colour nouns: brightness, depth, finish, hue, opacity, radiance.
Colour verbs: blaze, burn, clash, darken, embellish, sparkle.

Rayne Hall's *Writing Vivid Descriptions* provides structures for crafting evocative colour descriptions. For example:

Noun + colour: ash-grey, chocolate-brown, glacier-white.
Noun + 'coloured': blood-coloured, eggshell-coloured.
'the colour of' + adjective + noun: the colour of fallen snow.
Simile 'as' : as white as a bleached bedsheet.
Simile 'like': the autumn leaves looked like scattered gold coins.

Colour affects our mood. Think about the dreariness of a colourless winter. A cloud layer hung over London for the entire three weeks I was there one winter. The buildings were neutral-coloured, the people wore dark coats, and many trees were deciduous. It looked like a black-and-white photo. It was dull, dull, depressingly dull. By comparison, a typical Sydney winter's day has a bright cornflower-blue sky and a chill breeze. It is crisp yet invigorating.

We can influence a reader's mood by the words we link with colours. For example: 'Their seasick faces were as green as mushy peas'. Compare the difference in our readers' likely emotional response if we said: 'Her sparkling eyes were as green as polished emeralds.'

Light and darkness

A variation on colour is *light*. In our ancestors' time, light came from the sun, moon, stars, campfires, hearth fires, candles, lanterns, torches and, later, gas lights. The light was outside, inside or came through windows and doors. Here are some of its features:

Colour: white, yellow, orange, red, plus sunset tones.

Warmth: hot, warm, cool or cold.

Intensity: harsh, glaring, bright, intense, gentle, soft, muted.

The time of day is also relevant:

Morning: cool and clear, bright colours, crisp outlines, long shadows.

Midday: harsh, intense, washed-out colours, short shadows.

Late afternoon: warmer, softer, lengthening shadows.

Sunset: varies through yellow, orange, red, pink, lilac and grey.

Night-time: spears of moonlight, flickering shadows.

The amount of light influences mood. Daylight can be *cheery* and night-time *gloomy* and *sinister*. It is easy to communicate atmospheres of suspense and foreboding when writing about night-time events, especially if there is little light because of clouds or moonlessness.

Additionally, verbs associated with light describe what it shows and what it does:

Shows: reveals, illuminates, lights up.

Does: brushes, flickers, flares, glows, peeks, pierces, spills.

Rayne Hall in *Writing Vivid Settings* provides a guide to structuring sentences communicating light:

Warmth/intensity/colour + verb + place (+ verb + noun): The bright light spilled through the window and painted shadows on the floor.

Summary

Family histories must include visual descriptions of some sort, those that portray the setting if not the individual. As we have all heard: a picture tells a thousand words.

11

Sound

Noises surround us. As I sit here writing this section of the book, I can hear the hum of the computer and the purr of the cat sprawled across my desk. When I move near the window, I can hear birds' tweeting and leaves rustling in the gentle breeze.

Family histories rarely mention noises. Their silence suggests that our ancestors' world was silent. But it wasn't. We are instantly transported there when we read the following:

Hooves clattered across the cobblestones.

Let's again burrow down to find the foundational words and concepts that trigger our thoughts. General noise words relate to volume and harmoniousness:

Volume
Loudness: noisy, blaring, piercing, booming, thunderous.
Softness: quiet, gentle, light, soothing, peaceful, tranquil.

Harmoniousness
Pleasantness: lyrical, melodious, musical, tuneful, sweet.
Unpleasantness: discordant, cacophonous, harsh, raucous, shrill.

Think of these words when describing a place and its wildlife. We can refer to the countryside in general or to a feature of the countryside: a river, forest or farm. We can also use these words when describing a city, town, village, seaport or railway station. At a seaport we might hear the raucous squabbles of seagulls, the shrill curses of the dock-workers and the honks of departing ships.

There are two types of noises in our ancestors' world: background noises and action noises. These are discussed below.

Background noises

Background noises are divided into two types: inside noises and outside noises.

> The hearth fire crackled.

These words also transport us into our ancestor's home. What other household noises might we hear? The rattling of pots and pans. The whistle of a kettle. The miaows of cats and the cries of children.

For outside noises, think about the occupations in our ancestor's town or village and the resulting sounds that would have filled the air. In *How Surnames Began*, C.M. Matthews provides descriptions of town and country life with the aim of showing how surnames developed; we could use these descriptions to remind us of the occupations of the time. Or we could find children's books that describe town or village life in the past or read historical classics by authors such as Charles Dickens.

In describing background noises, don't just provide lists. Don't write, 'They were surrounded by the noises of town life.' Or 'They could hear the sounds of cows and horses.' Instead, use verbs to describe the actual noises. As I mentioned in *Writing Interesting Family Histories*, verbs are our action words. Verbs give our writing oomph.

My word bank of noises includes the following 'b' words, all of which are verbs:

> Babble, bang, bark, bash, bawl, bay, beep, bellow, blare, blast, bleat, bleep, blubber, boom, bray, bump, burble, burp, bustle, buzz.

When we focus on these words we are reminded of an obvious person or animal or thing that generates the noise. A river babbles. A door bangs. A dog barks. And so on. Start with the obvious then be more creative.

If our ancestors were migrants, think about the noises that surrounded them at their place of departure or arrival. I communicated the sounds of an 1840s railway station when I commenced *Peculiar Case*:

> Paddington Station was the usual whirl of noise and activity on New Year's Day 1845 as travellers prepared to board the Great Western Railway's steam trains, the iron horses that thundered across the countryside westward to Bristol. Bells pealed, passengers scrambled into carriages, porters stuffed cases into luggage vans, doors clanged, flags flapped, the locomotive chugged slowly from the station, the visitors hastened from the platform, and for a moment, too short a moment, there was blessed silence ...

This description not only communicates the sounds of a railway station, it generates a sense of action and energy. Think about the difference between the energy level in the above and in the usual family history style: 'John and Mary went by train from London to Bristol.'

Action noises

Action noises refer to the sounds we generate as we go about our daily lives. Humans generate two type of noises: vocal and physical.

Vocal

Vocalisations are the speech sounds we make; however, all of the sounds we emit from our mouths and noses are relevant to writers. As I looked through my word bank of noises to find examples, I was astonished to find nineteen starting with the letter 's' alone:

> Scream, screech, shout, shriek, sigh, sing, snap, snarl, snicker, sniff, sniffle, snigger, snivel, snort, snuffle, sob, squawk, squeak, squeal.

Again, these are all verbs and their use adds strength to our writing. Think of the difference between the following:

> The porter said to them ...

> The porter snapped at them ...

It is best not to overuse these types of words as *dialogue tags* (the descriptors attached to sentences of dialogue which are discussed in more detail in *Writing Interesting Family Histories*). It can seem melodramatic if we write: 'I am writing a family history,' she shrieked.'

Physical

Everything we do generates a noise of some sort. As I sit here writing these sentences, my fingers are tapping at the keyboard and every so often I reach over to click the mouse.

My word bank includes many noises we generate as we go about our daily life, including:

> Bump, crash, hammer, honk, jangle, knock, pound, rattle, ring, rustle, scrape, slap, slosh, smack, thump, tinkle.

We bump into a table. We crash into a garbage bin. We hammer a nail. We honk a horn. We jangle coins. And so on.

Writing 'sound' descriptions

In *Writing Interesting Family Histories* I talk about active and passive sentences. 'Sarah was baptised' is a passive sentence whereas 'The clergyman baptised Sarah' is an active sentence that better describes what actually happened.

When we write active sentences – when we attempt to *show* rather than *tell* – we are more likely to include physical actions along with the sounds these actions make. Compare the difference:

> Sarah was baptised …

> The clergyman *splashed* water over Sarah's forehead and *intoned* the words that …

Active sentences not only reflect the reality of the experience, they more easily communicate the sensory experiences – the sights, sounds and smells – that add life to our narrative. These sensory descriptions also help to progress our story in an interesting way.

12

Smell

Imagine if our ancestor was travelling in a stage coach across America and stopped in a town in the early hours of the evening. Cherie Priest in *Ganymede* sets the scene by providing a description based on smells:

> The night smelled of gun oil and saddles, and the jasmine colognes of night ladies, and the violets and azaleas that hung from balconies in baskets.

Anyone writing about America in the 1800s has a whole genre of books – westerns – to help them write vivid descriptions. When I was writing about bushranger Captain Thunderbolt, I borrowed some westerns from the local library to help me gain a sense of the world as seen from the saddle. The best westerns have evocative descriptions as well, so make the most of them.

The sense of smell is psychologically the most powerful of all of our senses because it links most closely to our memories. Researchers have determined that after three months we retain only 30% of our visual memory yet we still retain 100% of our olfactory memory after a year. My grandmother died when I was six yet, whenever I think of her, I smell violets. She used to wear violet-scented talc or perfume.

Thus, a reference to the smells of a place can be more effective in communicating its essence than a detailed visual description. Here is a perfect example from Rayne Hall's *Writing Vivid Settings*:

> The kitchen smelled of coffee, cinnamon and freshly-baked bread.

Who cares about its size or colour or position in the house? Our readers are immediately transported into the kitchen by that simple description of its smells.

Devon Monk's description of a riverside setting in *Magic to the Bone* could be used as a foundation for family historians writing about an ancestor who lived near a seaport or who travelled somewhere by sea.

> I took a couple of deep breaths, smelled rain, diesel and the pungent dead-fish-and-salt stench of the river.

Because smells trigger emotions, we should use pleasing smells when we want to communicate a positive emotion and unpleasant odours if we want to communicate a negative emotion.

Nice smells

Writing Vivid Descriptions provides an extremely useful guide to structuring sentences focusing on scents. For example, the pleasant 'kitchen' description above used the following structure:

> The place/air smelled of xx and yy and zz.

Other structures are:

> The scents/smells of xx and yy greeted her.

> The air was rich with the scents of xx and yy and zz.

My bank of words relating to nice smells includes: aroma, bouquet, fragrance, perfume, piquant, sweet.

Nasty smells

We can replace *smell* with a word like *stank* to communicate an unpleasant smell.

> The place stank of xx and yy.

> Or:

> The scent of xx failed to hide the stench of yy.

My bank of words associated with nasty smells includes: malodorous, noisome, odour, reeked, stank/stink, stench.

Writing smell descriptions

It is best to describe smells when a person arrives at a place so it forms part of the scene-setting component. We don't have to refer to smells alone. We could refer to something visual and two smells. Or to a noise and two smells. Or vice-versa. Patterns of 'three' work well in writing.

I had fun attempting to use Rayne Hall's structures to communicate smells in my latest book. For example, before reading her book, I had merely written that Chubbie went up to an artist's studio. Afterwards, I attempted to immerse myself in Chubbie's world and to imagine the reality of her olfactory experience:

> As he opened his door, the heady odour of paint and turpentine wafted towards them.

These structures make it surprisingly easy to craft 'smell' descriptions. Again, we need to be *showing* our biographical subjects living their stories rather than *telling* our readers what they are doing for this to work most effectively.

13

Taste

The sense of taste is the one we are least likely to use in a family history. Probably our most likely usage is if an ancestor moved between countries with completely different culinary styles; for example, if our ancestor emigrated from China to America.

Perhaps we could also refer to food experiences if our ancestors were in a confined area for a long time – say if they were forced to eat salted food during a long sea voyage. Or if they lived in or moved to an area when produce was limited. Many Irish peasants lived on little more than highly nutritious potatoes, which is why the potato blight was so catastrophic. Yet how many family historians documenting the lives of Irish migrants who fled from their homeland around the time of the potato famines actually write about the food situation from a taste and nutrition perspective in addition to the economic and social problems.

The sense we call *taste* is the most complex of all of our senses because it is the single sense that draws in all the others. The sense of taste doesn't merely refer to *taste*. It also refers to *flavour*. These are discussed separately below.

Taste sensations

If we have reason to refer to taste, it is helpful to know that we have five taste sensations: sweetness, sourness, saltiness, bitterness and umani. The latter is a Japanese loanword which can be translated as a 'pleasant savoury taste'. Taste words that might trigger our thoughts include:

Spiciness: chilli, curry, fiery, hot, peppery, spicy, tangy, zesty.
Saltiness: brackish, briny, saline.

Sourness: acidic, acrid, biting, bitter, sharp, tart, vinegary.
Sweetness: honeyed, saccharine, sugary, syrupy.
Umani: savoury.

Flavour sensations

Flavour is the impression that combines all the senses: taste, smell, texture, temperature, colour, shape and appearance.

An important element in the culinary world is the appearance of food. Layout has become an artform. And the smell, of course, is critical to enjoyment. Is it *mouth-watering* or *nauseating*? Then there are the sounds as we eat food, not just the *crunch* of the food itself, but the *slurp* of a drink or the *clatter* of crockery. We draw on the sense of touch both when we prepare food by hand and when we eat it, when it slides through our lips and onto our tongue. Finally, there is the critical issue of how it makes us emotionally feel. Many of our celebrations involve food.

Here are some word groups associated with flavour sensations:

Nature: buttery, cheesy, citrusy, creamy, fishy, fruity, garlicky.
Flavourfulness: flavoursome, piquant, tasty.
Flavourlessness: bland, insipid, mellow, mild, plain, tasteless.
Texture: chalky, chewy, crispy, crumbly, crunchy, crusty.
Temperature: hot, scorching, scalding, warm, tepid, cool, cold, icy.
Colour: as elsewhere.
Shape: as elsewhere.
Appearance: descriptions often involve similes and metaphors.
Problems: burnt, overripe, soggy, stale, tough, watery.

What generally matters most about taste sensations is what we *feel* about the flavour. Is it:

Nice: appetising, delectable, delicious, scrumptious, yummy.
Nasty: disgusting, foul, horrid, nauseating, sickening, vile.

Writing 'taste' descriptions

If our ancestors received an award at a big function, it might be appropriate to bring in the smell of food as part of our scene-setting description. Imagine our ancestor walking into the function room. Try to communicate what he might have seen and heard and smelt. For the latter, we could refer to the fragrances of perfumes and flowers and, of course, the food smells wafting towards him. A character in our story doesn't need to specifically taste food for us to obtain an impression through the description of its smell.

But, you might say, we don't know what food they served. There's a simple answer. We have a lot more food varieties today yet how often does the food at a function resemble the food at all the other functions we've attended. Chicken or beef for the main meal. A cake or other sugary item for desert. Wine, beer and juice. Tea and coffee.

When Chubbie was flying across America in the Powder Puff Derby of 1929, the derbyists were given fried chicken at every luncheon and dinner on their nine-day flight. Before their final banquet, they sent a message to the organisers saying that they would eat anything for dinner, anything but fried chicken!

Taste words and human character

Importantly, most words that relate to taste and flavour can also be applied to human character. She had a *fiery* personality. His expression was as *sour* as if he had sucked on lemons. Taste words can be used as character adjectives (*saccharine*) and as metaphors and similes.

Be creative.

14

Touch

Taste and touch are the most intimate of the senses because they require us to be in direct contact with the object we are tasting and touching. While we can see, hear and smell from a distance, both taste and touch are up-close-and-personal experiences.

The words *touch* and *feel* are often used interchangeably. I have separated them here so that *touch* refers to the physical sensation, which is discussed in this chapter, and *feel* to the emotional, which is discussed in the next chapter.

The sense of *touch* takes two forms: what we touch and what touches us.

What we touch

The most common style of family history writing is so distant in voice that it is hard to imagine our ancestors interacting physically with anything in their environment. Indeed, in most family histories, our ancestors managed to have half-a-dozen children without the slightest physical interaction with their spouses.

In the real world, it is impossible for us to not touch something – with one part of our body at least – at any given moment in time. As I write this, my bottom is sitting on a desk chair, my feet are resting on a footstool, my elbows are intermittently touching the table and my fingers are tapping at the keyboard. The only way in which we can't touch something physical is if we are gravity-less in space (which is intimated in family histories that fail to anchor their characters in a setting).

Think about all the things we touch in a day – and all the things our ancestors must have touched as they cooked, cleaned, washed, farmed, milked and so on. Obviously, most of us are not going to write too much about our ancestors' daily lives, although if there was something in their day that intrigued us it could become the subject of one of the story boxes discussed in chapter seventeen.

In an earlier chapter, we talked about examining our timeline entries to see if there was anything that could be used to tell a story. A journey is an obvious story. I started the 'Smell' chapter with a reference to a stagecoach trip. Think of the things our ancestor would have touched during such a trip. The feeling of her luggage as she carried it to the depot, of the hand that helped her up the stage-coach steps, of the wooden stage-coach door and architrave, of the seat she sat on. Think about how she might have been thrown against the wooden walls and might have clung to the curtains as the coached lurched through potholes. Every moment of her trip would have been a *touching* experience.

Again, here are some word groups to help drill down to the fundamentals.

Animacy: alive or dead; moving or stationary.

Size: tall, small, wide, narrow.

Firmness: soft or hard.

Roundness: flat, round or angular.

Texture: smooth or rough.

Sharpness: sharp or blunt.

Temperature: hot, warm, cool or cold.

Wetness: dry or wet.

We could write about someone who was about to undertake a sea journey:

> She reached out and grabbed the *moist* rail of the ship's ramp, worn *smooth* by the thousands of hands that had preceded hers.

What touches us

When we refer to the word *touch*, we tend to think of ourselves in the driving seat. We are the touchers and we interact with our world in this physical way. We touch a door to open it. We hold and stroke a child. We kiss a lover. We cook a meal.

Alternatively, we are touched by something that is concrete and physical: a person, a leaf or branch, a door that slams on us. When we talk about being touched by something else, the words listed in the 'What we touch' section remain relevant.

We are also touched every day by something more ethereal: the atmosphere around us.

Think about how we interact with our environment. Sydney in February is hot and humid. How unpleasant it must have been for our female ancestors in their ankle-length, many-layered dresses as their sweat made the fabric cling to them. Their attire was ideal for an English winter but not an Australian summer.

To write about the environment and the way it would have felt to our ancestors, here are some trigger words:

Temperature: scorching, hot, warm, cool, cold, freezing.

Humidity: dry, moist, humid.

Wetness: raining, snowing, sleeting, hailing.

Windiness: windy, gusty, blustery, calm, still.

Writing 'touch' descriptions

It is easy to communicate a sense of the atmosphere. We could write about the *crisp coldness* of a winter morning or the *icy sting* of a winter's wind or the *clamminess* of a hot humid day. Remember: while a thermometer might tell us that the air is cold or hot, the phrases *crisp coldness* and *icy sting* and *clamminess* refer to our own physical sensations – or those of our ancestors – as the atmosphere touches us.

Using these types of phrases draws our reader into our ancestors' world without the need to write long sentences or paragraphs of descriptive prose.

15

Emotionally feel

Which affects us the most? The factual things that happen to us or our emotional responses? The answer is simple. Unless it is something as dramatic as a bus crashing into us, it is usually our emotional responses. This explains why some people can survive trauma with little ongoing effect and others are psychologically destroyed by it.

Emotions dominate our lives. As I sit here typing these words I feel joy because I love writing. I also feel some tension and frustration because of the fifteen items on my task list that need to be completed today (I would prefer to keep writing). I feel delight at the thought of going on holidays in three weeks yet stress at the thought of my pre-holiday task list. More emotions are added when I think about the work pressure my husband is under, my daughter's new job opportunity, my son's new relationship, and the cat's determination to keep walking across my keyboard.

All of us swing between emotions: small swings for calm personalities, big swings for volatile personalities. Yet most genealogists steer clear of any references to their ancestors' emotions when they write their family histories.

Why? Because they think they don't know what their ancestors felt. Yet what should be clear from the above paragraph is that we feel many things at the same time. Moreover, psychologists have determined that we have a surprisingly small number of different emotions. So all we have to do is to mentally put ourselves in our ancestor's shoes, think about how we would feel under the circumstances and (so long as we don't have a phobia or a psychopathic personality disorder) communicate the range of emotions we would feel. Because it is extremely likely that this range of emotions will cover the emotions our ancestors would also have felt.

Different individuals and organisations group emotions differently. Here is a list of emotion groups, each of which contains a range of emotions from mild to extreme.

Happiness: pleasure, amusement, delight, joy, merriment.

Sadness: sorrow, gloom, misery, wretchedness, devastatation.

Love: fondness, affection, adoration, lust, love, passion, desire.

Hate: aversion, dislike, distaste, contempt, disgust, revulsion.

Anger: annoyance, irritation, vexation, fury, rage.

Suspicion: doubt, distrust, wariness, disbelief, apprehension.

Fear: anxiety, nervousness, tension, fright, panic, terror.

Hope/trust: confidence, anticipation, optimism, faith, belief.

Surprise: wonder, disbelief, astonishment, amazement.

Jealousy/greed: envy, covetousness, avariciousness, greed.

Insecurity: hesitance, self-doubt, timidity, shyness.

Shame/guilt: embarrassment, remorse, humiliation, self-reproach.

Pride: arrogance, smugness, conceit, self-importance, vanity.

Humility: humbleness, modesty, self-effacement, meekness.

Boredom: tediousness, ennui, monotonousness.

Interest: curiosity, awareness, attentiveness.

Relief: a sense of release, respite, reprieve.

Family historians who refer to emotions tend to use qualifiers: 'She probably felt …' or 'We can imagine that she felt …' These types of descriptions make it seem as if the author is intruding into the tale. They also seem clumsy and can make a reader cringe.

Writing active rather than passive prose – that is, when we *show* our characters living their own stories rather than *tell* the reader what they have done – is the only way to communicate emotions effectively. This is because, if we *tell* readers what our characters have done, we are forced to *tell* readers what our characters have felt. And if we won't give ourselves permission to say it outright – 'she felt excited' – we are forced to qualify any statement we make – 'she probably felt excited'. That's why it seems so clumsy.

Writing 'feeling' descriptions

How can we communicate emotions without specifically referring to them? When I wrote the following paragraph I knew that Chubbie was a Melbourne housewife who liked to party; that she was on a solo holiday in London; that she was about to return to Australia by plane; that she and the pilot had been farewelled at a party in Murray's Night Club in Soho in October 1927 (information about the club was accessible via the internet); and that she wouldn't return to London for five years. I wanted to communicate excitement, both in terms of the party and the big picture. I also wanted to communicate a sense of impending doom.

> There among the glitz and glamour of cabaret London, as they twirled under the chandeliers to the jittery beat of the latest dance jingles, she had her last taste of the exhilarations of 1920s London. The vibrant city – indeed the entire world – would be vastly different by the time she returned.

This paragraph is filled with energy and emotion. It communicates a sense of Chubbie's excitement yet at no point does it specifically say what she was feeling.

Summary

These last six chapters have communicated one of the most important ingredients of writing a gripping story: drawing upon sensory impressions to communicate our ancestors' world. When I ask family history writing students about the differences between novels and encyclopaedias, someone usually refers to descriptions involving the senses. This indicates that they come readily to mind so it shouldn't be too hard to make the most of these suggestions.

16

Character and Personality

The phrase 'actions speak louder than words' is one we should remember when we explore our ancestors' lives. Professional biographers use their subject's words and deeds to assess personality and character. We should do the same.

An article 'Personality vs. Character' by Dr Alex Lickerman on the *Psychology Today* website explains the difference between the two:

> Personality is easy to read, and we're all experts at it. We judge people funny, extroverted, energetic, optimistic, confident— as well as overly serious, lazy, negative, and shy—if not upon first meeting them, then shortly thereafter ... Character, on the other hand, takes far longer to puzzle out. It includes traits that reveal themselves only in specific—and often uncommon— circumstances, traits like honesty, virtue, and kindliness.

Personality traits are mostly hereditary and unchangeable whereas character is based upon beliefs that can be changed, albeit with difficulty.

There are five primary personality traits: openness to experience, conscientiousness, extraversion, agreeableness, and neuroticism or emotional stability. Google 'big five personality traits' for more information. Various websites also include hundreds of words describing personality and character traits. These include:

Positive: active, adaptable, adventurous, alert, amiable, articulate.

Neutral: absentminded, ambitious, amusing, authoritarian.

Negative: abrasive, abrupt, aimless, aloof, amoral, angry, anxious.

Personality and character drive behaviour. So how can we use our ancestors' actions to gain a sense of who they were as individuals?

Migrants

Our ancestors didn't migrate to another country simply because, for example, Britain's enclosure laws meant that they were kicked off their land and were struggling to survive. They migrated because, of all the options available to them – changing to a different occupation, sleeping on a relative's couch, begging, theft, prostitution – emigration seemed like the optimal solution. This decision also meant that, on the timidity/courage spectrum, courage won. How many people remained 'at home' and struggled to survive for the rest of their lives because they lacked the courage to make such a life-changing move?

Of course, some members of a migrating family group might have had little or no say in the decision-making process: submissive spouses, children, elderly parents whose entire family was migrating. Each would have experienced his or her own set of emotions, including trust that others were making the right decision mixed with trepidation and perhaps excitement.

Think about what we would have felt in these different types of situations and ask others what they would have felt. This is important because different personalities react differently to the same situation. I once listened to a podcast during a car trip with my mother. I am an optimistic social progressive whereas my mother is a pessimistic social conservative. My response, which was directed at a third person in the car, was 'Sounds great. Go for it.' My mother's was, 'That sounds dreadful. Forget it.'

Criminals

There was an attitude in the past, one still held by many today, that people resort to crime out of choice. Those holding such a view cannot know much about history and criminology. In fact, our ancestors usually resorted to crime – even murder – because it seemed the optimal solution to whatever problem they faced.

One of the fascinating lessons from the 'Australia experiment' was that, once Britain's criminals were transported to the other side of the world and discovered that they had good weather, food, jobs and opportunities (many well-behaved convicts received land grants), most became law-abiding members of society. In fact, convicts began telling their friends and families in Britain and Ireland to commit crimes so as to get transported to Australia because they would be much better off than in their homeland. The authorities' response, naturally, was a complete failure to recognise the social and economic point being made and, instead, to make the punishments for crime harsher.

These days we have a deeper understanding of criminality as a reflection of genetic, psychological and social factors. Thus, anyone interested in understanding the character of our criminal ancestors should read books about history and about criminology.

The religious

For many of our ancestors, the only documentary evidence attesting to their existence is their appearance in church registers. Let's say that our English ancestor lived in a country town in the 1800s and was baptised in the established (Anglican) church. Does this mean that his or her parents were devoutly religious? Not at all.

In order to understand what religious affiliation tells us about our ancestors' characters, we need first to understand religion as a political and social entity. Historical, psychological, sociological and anthropological research provides fascinating insights into religions and religious belief. Religions began in pre-scientific societies as a means of explaining the universe, controlling society and controlling individual behaviour. The belief that people were being watched by a supreme being and would be rewarded or punished for their behaviour was a powerful coercive. The principle behind CCTV cameras is much the same.

Psychologists today recognise that religious adherence is primarily a function of 'arbitrary coherence' – that is, we adopt to a greater or lesser degree the religious, political, philosophical and cultural views of the family/society we were arbitrarily born or adopted into, along with the language, clothing and music styles. Census returns show a much larger number of people who tick 'yes' to a specific religious allegiance than regularly attend a place of worship because of this cultural adherence.

Why are some people more pious than others? Psychologists recognise that the degree of piety is a function of a belief system's ability to meet the needs of the believer, whether it is for the emotional and psychological comfort the religion brings, the sense of community, the social contacts, and so on.

So how is this relevant for genealogists? Suppose we have an ancestor who was baptised in an Anglican church, and whose siblings remained with the established church, yet this ancestor chose to join a non-conformist church (Methodists, Congregationalists, Baptists, Quakers and so on). What does this tell us? It serves as evidence that something about that non-conformist faith pulled our ancestor towards it because it seemed likely to meet his or her psychological and emotional needs.

Of course, it is important to conduct background research rather than make shallow assumptions. A move to a new location might have planted our ancestors in a place where the family's faith was not represented, leading them to choose a local church whose views and practices were similar.

Obviously, our first challenge is to read the history of this new religion or denomination, both generally and in relation to the area in which our ancestor lived. It is also important to remember that piety is a double-edged sword with bigotry its uglier face. The Quakers, for example, broke away from the established church in the mid-1600s and were persecuted by members of the established church to the point of imprisonment and execution. Thus, we should also try to determine the broader community's reaction to people who broke from one faith and joined another so as to ascertain if our ancestors might have been ostracised for doing so. For example, the more pious the family, the less willing they are to accept a family member who breaks with tradition.

Our ancestor's willingness to change faith also opens a window into his or her character and personality. Think about the possibilities. Does it suggest open-mindedness to new ideas or perhaps gullibility? If an ancestor joined a non-conformist church and also joined the masses heading to the 'new world' (Australia, America, Canada), this could suggest a 'grass is greener' mentality as both the 'push' and 'pull' factors, although it could also indicate that the person was being 'pushed' from their homeland because of their new faith.

Of course, the psychological yearning that led to a change of faith might have been more pragmatic. It might have been focused on a member of the opposite sex who attended the place of worship.

Ask ourselves 'Why?'

Skilled genealogists tend to ask the 'why?' question in terms of the 'push' and 'pull' social factors relating to our ancestors' lives; however, few seem to ponder the psychological or character-based factors. This is extraordinary because our actions are primarily driven by our psychological needs and desires. If we want to fully understand behaviour we need to seek insights into character. So remember that phrase 'character drives behaviour' and try to seek answers so we can offer our readers insights and enlightenment.

Communicating character and personality

In the previous chapter, I mentioned that family historians who refer to their ancestors' emotions tend to use qualifiers: 'She probably felt ...' or 'We can imagine that she felt ...'. The same is true on the rare occasions when family historians communicate character.

Similarly to communicating feelings, it is only when we *show* our biographical subjects living their own stories, rather than *tell* the reader what they have done, that we can communicate character and personality effectively. This is because, if we *tell* readers what our biographical subjects have done, we are forced to *tell* readers what this says about them.

Communicating character and personality is best done with subtlety. Here is an extract from the start of *Chubbie Miller*. It communicates a sense of Chubbie's personality by its description of London in the mid-1920s:

> Yet it was the atmosphere of flapper London that proved so unexpected, so at odds with her father's fond memories of a Victorian England. The 'bright young things' who dashed around London in their loose glittery dresses and daring knee-high skirts

had not only abandoned the Victorian constraints of corset and crinoline, of piety and prudery, they had embraced the sensual. Their adventurous flamboyance expressed an intoxicating independence, an uncaging of body and soul. This freedom represented the dawn of a new era, with London as its epicentre, the quintessence of modernity.

It couldn't have been more different to the constrained and insular world she had come from, the world that was dragging her back as each day of her six-month holiday ticked away.

If this doesn't tell you that she craved freedom and excitement, I don't know what does. Yet at no point does it specifically say so.

The rest of the book confirms it. The very fact that she climbed back into that flimsy biplane and kept flying after the disasters that befell her *shows* the most extraordinary courage. The word 'courage' never needed to be mentioned.

Summary

It is easier to determine personality and character, to some degree at least, than most of us realise. In the same way that we can step into an ancestors' shoes and try to work out what they were probably feeling at the time of a specific event, we can get a sense of their characters and personalities by their responses to the specific event.

Sure, we might not be able to say much, if anything at all, about a person for whom we only have baptism, marriage and burial references in the established church register. On the other hand, we could probably argue that they were conformists, without a strong need to rebel against the system (see: once we start assessing personality and character, it's hard not to come up with something).

Humans do not have only a single personality trait. We have many. Common sense will provide many of the answers. And it's better to offer something reasonable than ignore the subject altogether.

17

Story boxes

Many genealogists struggle with the idea of writing gripping prose that reads as if our biographical subjects are living their own stories. I can understand that. It took many years of writing practise for me to break free from the old genealogical style of fact-focused writing. If you read my first book, *An Irresistible Temptation* (2006), then read my sixth book, *Chubbie Miller* (2017), you would be astonished at the difference in writing style. *Temptation* reads like interesting non-fiction. *Chubbie* reads like gripping fiction.

So how can we write gripping family histories if we are unable to move beyond the style 'Sarah Adams was born on 1 February 1799 at Deal, Kent, England to John Adams ...'? Since I wrote *Writing Interesting Family Histories*, I've had a number of great ideas, one being 'story boxes'.

My idea of story boxes incorporates ideas that came from two other authors. First, I helped an author named Jane Smith with her children's book about Thunderbolt. When I saw the finished publication, it reminded me that children's books often have text-boxes scattered around the page that contain stories or jokes or fun facts or other snippets.

Second, I read a memoir called *A Brush with Mondrian* by Yvonne Louis, which told the story of her search for the origins of Dutch paintings held by her family. At various places in the book, the story was told through the eyes of the characters in the paintings. This led me to think about different perspectives – different voices – and how they could be communicated

Here is my suggestion. Imagine a page in a family history. On one section of the page – for example, on the right-hand side – we have the ongoing fact-driven family history. On the other side, we have a text box in which we include other information about the individual or the family.

What do we include in the boxes? There are many possibilities. The most obvious is to include peripheral information – for example, details about an immigrant ship, or a weather event in our ancestor's vicinity, or some other local drama – the type of information we would prefer not to include in a biography as it might bog down narrative. However, my aim here is to show how we can include other voices in our family history.

1. The person's own voice

Perhaps we have a letter from our biographical subject. It might contain information we want to include in our biography. However, it might also be relevant as a means of hearing our ancestor's writing voice. When I researched Captain Thunderbolt, I discovered that he regularly started sentences with the word 'Well'. It enabled me to confirm that he was responsible for a bushranging incident about which there was some uncertainty.

When we read an ancestor's written words, we can determine their level of education via their sentence structure and phraseology, and we can gain a picture of them as a person. This type of assessment can be as interesting as reading the contents themselves. Some family historians include a scanned copy of such letters in the publication; however, young people today are brought up with typescript writing and cannot read such letters, and most other people are time-poor and unwilling to devote much energy to deciphering them. Additionally, the letters may include information that is tedious and irrelevant.

By typing the important details into a text box, we can communicate the relevant information as a separate voice without boring the reader with the peripheral information. And we can include a snippet of the letter elsewhere as an image or picture so the reader can see our ancestor's writing.

2. A family voice

Perhaps we are writing a biography about a male ancestor and want to include a letter or letters his wife wrote to him. We don't want to incorporate the information into the factual biography; instead, we want our readers to hear the contents of the letters as if they were spoken by a separate voice. Again, we can include this information in a story box.

3. A friendly voice

We might have a letter from a family friend, or a newspaper account from an old-timer who mentions our family, or some other distant source of information. We can include the contents in our family history without incorporating them in our ancestor's biography.

4. A story-telling voice

After I wrote a book about the bushranger Captain Thunderbolt, many people mentioned that they had family stories about their ancestor's encounters with the 'gentleman bushranger'. Family stories, particularly those that are impossible to verify and those that seem spurious, are perfect for story boxes.

*

All of the above 'voices' contain information provided by our biographical subject or their friends and family members. There are other voices and perspectives that could be included in the story boxes. What about hearing from us as the researcher and writer?

5. The author's voice

Most genealogists omit the details of their research discoveries when they write their family histories. Yet taking the reader on our own journey of discovery will often be the most exciting – and memorable – part of our family history. We should make a point of documenting how we stumbled across exciting information soon after it happened for the purposes of including it in a family history. Or we could write about some of our more dramatic research activities. As a 22-year-old, I resorted to hitch-hiking on my own in Scotland, as the afternoon light dimmed, to get to a graveyard. Can you hear the ominous background music? Fortunately, I lived to tell the tale. I think the man who picked me up was more scared of me than I was of him, but he couldn't bear to leave me in such a dangerous situation. When he heard what I was doing, he was so interested he took me the entire way to the graveyard.

6. A voice of complaint

Many of us have struggled to trace an ancestor and have cursed the person for being so difficult. We could write them a letter of complaint.

> Dear William,
> I am not the type of person who normally threatens people with physical violence, but if you weren't already dead …!

Add humour where possible. Our readers will be grateful.

*

We are now going to launch ourselves into the realms of the fictional imagination. Sometimes genealogists find it impossible to allow themselves to go beyond the dry facts when writing their family history yet they have a creative writing spirit that is willing to be released when they can make it clear that what they are writing is pure fiction. The following provide such opportunities.

7. A property's voice

What if our ancestors lived in the same property for generations? A place like Downton Abbey, for example. Or a farm or seaside cottage. The property should serve as a unifying theme in our family history. However, inexperienced writers might find it difficult to use a property as a narrative arc. It might be easier to include some information about the house in a story box.

We could be dryly factual, documenting when it was built and when it was added to or renovated and anything else that was factually relevant. Or we could imagine what the property might have seen over the decades or centuries and tell the story through the house's 'voice'. We could incorporate family information and background historical information. We could talk about the weather and what effect it had on the property; for example, it might be situated in the frozen wastes of Canada or the heat of outback Australia or the flooding areas of New Orleans.

One of my genealogical writing students had an American Civil War house in their family, one replete with bullets holes. To fail to have the house as a 'voice' in that family history would be a major loss for the house itself and for the student's readers. Seek the stories and maximise the drama, even if we choose to do so in a story box.

8. An heirloom's voice
In *A Brush with Mondrian*, the author told part of her family's story as if it were being seen by paintings that had travelled half-way around the world with her family. And the paintings did indeed *see* what was happening because they were attached to the walls of the family's residences.

Is there an heirloom of some sort that could be used as a 'voice' in our family history? A painting, a vase, a ring, a broach.

9. Our ancestor's voice
What if our ancestor fought in a war or lived through a dramatic time? We might not have enough information to include such an account in a rigidly factual section of the family history but be willing to explore possibilities in a story box.

10. A servant's voice
Has anyone read the book (or seen the movie) *The Help* by Kathryn Stockett? Imagine the story a servant could tell about the family who employed him or her. I can't imagine too many families being willing to air their dirty linen in such a way. However, the purpose here is to present ideas that might spur a 'Eureka' moment.

11. Anything else ...
A friend of mine loves domestic history. If she was using story boxes in her family history, she could include domestic history titbits that fascinate her. Similarly so, we could use a story box to include anything about our ancestor's life or world that we thought was relevant or that interested us. It is our family history and we can do whatever we want.

Visual layout

I am not going to discuss layout in this publication. I am a wordsmith not a book designer. That type of advice would be better sourced from a family historian who works for the design section of a publishing house.

My suggestion is to examine family histories and other image-heavy publications to see what aspects of the layout seem appealing. There are shelves and shelves of them in local libraries.

18

Editing titbits

There are lots of little things we need to know to help in our family history writing. These are discussed in the following pages.

Location anchoring

It is essential when we write our family histories that we anchor our ancestors in their location early on in the relevant biography. Afterwards, it is unnecessary to repeat the location information unless our biographical subject changes residence.

For example, in the full internet biography of Reverend Charles Rich (the fifth paragraph only was reproduced in chapter one), the author helpfully anchors his biographical subject in 'Camberwell, Surrey, England' in the second sentence of the first paragraph. Two sentences later, however, the author again refers to Camberwell as being in Surrey. This clarification is unnecessary because the reader already knows where Camberwell is situated.

In the biography's second paragraph, the author has his subject arriving in 1833 in 'Sydney'. The internet is accessible all over the world and there are other places named 'Sydney'; therefore the author should have written 'Sydney, New South Wales, Australia'. The author doesn't mention 'Australia' until the eighth sentence of the second paragraph and refers to 'Sydney, New South Wales' in the following sentence. If the author had properly anchored his subject at the start of the second paragraph, he could have omitted all later references to 'New South Wales, Australia' when referring to 'Sydney'.

Additionally, the author failed to appropriately anchor 'Pyrmont' and 'Paddington'. Both are suburbs of Sydney. If the author was attempting to write prose rather than list facts, he could have written:

> In the mid-1880s, Charles moved to "Elamang", Elizabeth Street, Paddington, a suburb of Sydney, where he resided for a couple of years.

Simple, explanatory and readable.

Timeframe anchoring

Genealogists flood their family histories with every date and other fact they have found. In *Writing Interesting Family Histories*, I talk about how facts are like hammer blows pounding away at a reader's brain. That's why we find it hard to finish reading a single encyclopaedia article let alone read an entire encyclopaedia.

In a family history, some dates act as timeframe anchors providing readers with a sense of when an event occurred. For example, it is important to list the full birth-date for our biographical subject. However, if we plan to include a timeline in our family history – as is strongly recommended – there is rarely any need to include the baptism date in our narrative because the full baptism details are included in the timeline. If we must mention the baptism, it is easier for our readers if we say that our biographical subject was baptised 'a week later' or 'two months later' or 'in the spring'.

Here is an example using the details for Sarah Adams. The fact-focused family historian writes:

> Sarah Adams was born in Deal, Kent, England on 1 February 1799 to John Adams, a blacksmith, and his wife Mary, nee Jones. She was baptised on 24 March 1799 at St Mary's Church of England, Deal.

This paragraph is cumbersome and tedious because it includes eight facts in two sentences. Of these, two are dates. Dates are among the hardest facts to read because they mostly comprise numbers rather than words.

As I stressed in *Writing Interesting Family Histories*, we must never ever start a family history, or a chapter in a family history, with a sentence like 'Sarah Adams was born ...'. That being the case, we will presume that a second narrative-driven author has already anchored the family in a specific location before writing:

Sarah Adams was born there on 1 February 1799 and baptised at the local Anglican church seven weeks later. Her father ...

It's much more readable, isn't it? Readability is so important that it is discussed in the section below.

If anyone is alarmed at the thought of not including the specifics about Sarah's date and place of baptism in the narrative, remember that they are in her timeline, which can be easily accessed by anyone who wants to know them. Let me make it clear, though, that most readers will have no interest in doing so. And those who *are* interested will find it incredibly helpful to have all of the facts about Sarah's life listed one after another in the timeline.

Genealogists should ensure that the facts – particularly the dates – listed in a family history do not just sit there in relative isolation but serve as stepping stones to something more interesting. If a writer includes a full date in a novel, for instance, the reader thinks that this information is being communicated because it is important and needs to be remembered. Most of the full dates listed in family histories do not serve as stepping stones. That being the case, the specificity of a full date when the date itself is unimportant acts like a 'cry wolf' moment. The reader soon encounters another full date that goes nowhere, then another. Before long, the reader realises that the writer has included all of these full dates for no other reason than that he or she has located them and has nowhere else to document them. The reader starts to skim over them. Once the skimming process begins, the reader skims over more and more of the prose until it becomes difficult to re-engage with the text. Eventually, the family history gets tossed aside.

If we include a timeline for each biographical subject – or biographical couple – in our family histories, we can eliminate most full dates from our narrative. For example, a descendant reading our narrative will rarely need to know that their ancestor bought a block of land on '2 June 1842'. As the details of the land purchase are listed in the timeline, it is more readable if we write that our ancestor bought the land in 'mid-1842' or in 'June 1842' or, unless the mid-year purchase is relevant for some reason, in

'1842'. By providing a looser date, we are telling the reader that we are merely anchoring the timeframe for them and that the date itself is otherwise unimportant. If we make a habit of using the broadest of timeframe anchors, the occasions when we do include a full date will signal to the reader that the date is important.

In chapter two, I wrote about the 'Killer Bullet' that my protagonist Chubbie was flying. I ended the chapter that preceded her disappearance with a single-sentence paragraph:

> At 9.11 am on Friday, 28 November 1930, Chubbie took off from Havana in her flame-red Bullet and headed towards the deep blue waters of the Florida Strait.

The specificity of the time and full date tells the reader that something is about to happen. It also generates a sense of foreboding, which is a great way of communicating tension, as dicussed in chapter eight.

Readability

The purpose of prose in a non-fiction book is to communicate information to a reader. However, some authors seem to have forgotten this simple goal. Instead, they seem more intent on impressing readers with their intelligence.

While I was researching capital punishment for *Black Widow*, I stumbled across a helpful book (Timothy Kauf-Osborn's *From Noose to Needle*) that is so 'badly' written – if clear communication is the yardstick measuring 'good' writing – that it provides 200 pages of brilliant 'how not to' examples. Here is one paragraph plucked at random from the book:

> Much the same end is achieved via the law's endorsement of a culturally specific construction of pain. That account, occluding its own historicity, renders pain radically solipsistic and so effectively unintelligible.

Seriously? It isn't 'pain' that is unintelligible but this academic's prose! It took me three days to decipher 200 pages and if the author was nearby I would have throttled him.

In the academic world, this type of prose can be considered clever. It isn't. Our purpose is to *communicate* with our readers. Our purpose is not to make them think how smart we are.

In fact, this type of writing is usually counter-productive because, instead of making readers think the writer is smart, it makes readers feel stupid because they can't understand what is being communicated. When readers feel stupid, they are more likely to chuck a book away and to refuse to read anything else written by the same author. It is also counter-productive because those who practise this type of obscure writing usually find it impossible to get mainstream book contracts even though they might have something worthwhile to say.

Compare the above with the prose of an academic who did succeed in obtaining such a contract. Emeritus Professor James Whorten wrote in *The Arsenic Century* (a fascinating book, by the way):

> Too indulgent, it would seem, much too indulgent for his own good, for despite seeing that she was 'educated with the utmost tenderness' and taking 'every possible care ... to impress her mind with sentiments of virtue and religion', Francis Blady reared a daughter so lacking in judgment as to be seduced by a scheming bounder into carrying out the murder of her own doting father.

Readability is one of the greatest gifts we can give our readers. If a family history reads like the Sarah Adams example on page 103, the author needs to do some serious thinking about writing style.

Positive and negative sentences

When I was studying first-year psychology, we were told that exam questions should always be phrased *positively* rather than *negatively* because research had shown that they are easier to comprehend. If only this information had been communicated to the third-year psychology lecturer who prepared our exam paper.

We too need to craft positive rather than negative sentences as much as possible. Here is a example of a negative sentence from a novel I once read. The italics are my own:

'I'm *not* a coroner who believes in restricting access to my enquiries.'

As the speaker was in fact a coroner, this is clearly a badly phrased sentence. How could it be improved? I tried sliding the negative component further along in the sentence.

'I'm a coroner who does *not* believe in restricting access to my enquiries.'

The problem with this restructured sentence is that it mentions a *non-belief* whereas the coroner is actually expressing a *belief*. She would be expressing a non-belief if she said, 'I'm a coroner who does not believe in fairies.' Let's try again.

'I'm a coroner who believes in *not* restricting access to my enquiries.'

This is still a negative sentence, one with a double negative in fact – *not restricting* – but at least it is more accurate in its substance. The positive sentence would be:

'I'm a coroner who believes in *allowing* access to my enquiries.'

Sometimes writers actually need to weaken the power of a positive sentence or communicate a negative slant. In those instances, a negative sentence serves the purpose. However, if a negative sentence is deliberately being used, make sure that the internal parts are structured accurately and logically.

Chronological and unchronological sentences
One of the reasons my writing style is easy to comprehend is because I structure sentences chronologically as much as possible. I'm not talking here about the chronological structure of a biography but rather the structure of the parts within a single sentence. Here are two examples in which the same information is structured differently but reflects a chronological progression:

Chubbie waved to the crowd then climbed into her plane.

After waving to the crowd, Chubbie climbed into her plane.

Both sentences are chronological although the second sounds more sophisticated. The second structure can be used to break up a paragraph full of sentences structured like the first sentence.

The third example breaks the chronological rule.

Chubbie climbed into her plane after waving to the crowd.

In breaking the chronological structure, it forces the reader to mentally zig-zag. The reader's mind is travelling in one direction, then it is forced to jump backwards in time to make sense of the sentence. It mentally rearranges the information then jumps forwards in time again.

Unchronological sentences have a jarring effect on a reader. If they are found regularly in a piece of prose, readers start to feel as if they are running a hurdle race.

During the editing phase, pay attention to those jarring sensations. Our brain is telling us that something is wrong and needs to be fixed.

Numbers

Different publishing companies have different ways of writing numbers. These days they seem to write full words for one to twenty and numbers thereafter: 21, 22, 23. Or they write full words for everything (apart from dates and times) unless it is cumbersome.

Try to maintain a consistent numbering strategy within an individual paragraph. It is inconsistent if we write: 'There are seven days in the week and 52 weeks in the year'.

Never start a paragraph with a numeric number unless it is a timeframe anchor at the start of a chapter as shown below:

1845, London:
Paddington Station was the usual whirl ...

In the prose section of a family history, or any other publication, instead of writing '1845 was the year when ...', it is better to rearrange the words so that it reads 'In the year 1845 ...'.

And instead of writing, '95 passengers stepped on board...', it is better to write 'Ninety-five passengers stepped on board ...'.

Currency

What do we do when we are dealing with currency in family histories? Do we provide the exact amount down to the halfpenny or do we round it for readability purposes?

If we publish a timeline in our family history, we can include the exact amount in the timeline. This allows us to round '£98 10s 3½d' to '£100' or to 'just under £100' in the body of our narrative. In the narrative, the exact price or value will generally cause our readers to stumble whereas a rounded figure will usually communicate the necessary information in a readable way. Occasionally, though, only the exact amount communicates the necessary point so this needs to be taken into consideration when dealing with numbers.

Do we provide an idea of the value of such an amount in today's currency? The problem with estimating value is that there are many different ways of doing so. The bank robbery haul in *Breaking the Bank* in 1828 was £14,000. As there are no Australian conversion rates for this period, I had to rely on British pound converters. The British estimates for this value varied enormously. Converted to Australian dollars, they were: $2.6 million using the Retail Price Index, $26 million using the wages conversion and $89 million using the Gross Domestic Product conversion. A book that valued Australia's richest people (William Rubenstein, *The All-Time Australian 200 Rich List*) estimated that £14,000 in 1828 was worth about $6 billion today.

Most conversions reflect the Retail Price Index (RPI). While this is probably useful for valuing bread or clothes or typical items found in the RPI's 'basket of goodies', it is unlikely to accurately reflect the value of property, businesses, capital or a huge bank haul.

Abbreviations

In the Charles Rich biography, the author refers to Charles' residence as 'Padd.', an abbreviation for Paddington. This is a literary no-no. Think carefully about abbreviations, both in terms of their readability and their aesthetic appearance. If the abbreviation is in common usage, like 'Mrs' or 'Dr', it is acceptable. If in doubt, write the word in full.

Errors

We all make errors. They are unavoidable. That's why mainstream publishers employ a proof-reader to run through a manuscript *after* it has already gone through three or more professional edits.

We find it hard to pick up all the typos in our own prose because we hear our sentences running through our brains like a melody line rather than actually seeing what we have written. It is always a good idea to have a fresh set of eyes peruse our writing. If we cannot access that type of assistance, take a few weeks' break from the prose – it's called giving ourselves *distance* – then read it again. It is amazing the number of errors we pick up when we allow time for the melody line to quieten.

Source referencing

If the author of the Charles Rich biography had annotated each sentence, or had provided a single grouped annotation at the end of each paragraph, he could have left out the phrase 'He was listed in a directory dated from …', which occurs an astonishing five times in the single paragraph.

Information about source-referencing techniques is provided in *Writing Interesting Family Histories*. Suffice it to say here that source-reference details should never be included in the narrative, unless of course we are quoting something or someone. If there is a disparity between information contained in different records, the analysis of the evidence should not be included in the main text. Rather, it should be included in a footnote or endnote. Do not bore readers with evidence analysis in the body of a biography.

Cut! Cut! Cut!

Publishers dislike writers who under-write because it is difficult to pad-out a publication and maintain dramatic tension and prose tightness. Publishers love writers who over-write because the cutting process improves the prose, tightens the narrative and increases the pace or tension.

When we self-publish a family history, words are money. Every additional page adds to the unit price we pay. Here is a strategy for cutting words from a family history.

1. Note down the total page length of the Word file and the total number of words written.
2. Calculate how many words need to be cut from each page. We should try to cut between ten and twenty percent.
3. Keep a log that notes the page number, the number of words on the page when the editing commenced, the number of words when the editing finished, the number of words needed to be cut, the number that have been cut, and the difference between the two. Monitoring our progress helps keep us motivated.
4. Make it a challenge to eliminate more words from each page than required. This often requires us to rewrite sentences, which tightens and improves the quality of the prose.

Professional or extremely experienced writers should aim to cut at least ten percent, inexperienced writers twenty percent or more. This is because inexperienced writers tend to write overly wordy sentences containing lots of unimportant words like prepositions and linking terms.

Family historians can also reduce wordiness by deleting unnecessary facts and repeated words. For example, the author of Charles Rich's biography would not only improve readability by cutting out the repeated use of the location anchor 'Sydney, New South Wales, Australia', he would also cut out words.

Producing pdfs

When we self-publish a family history, if we are typesetting the pages ourselves, we will need to send the printers a .pdf file. This is to ensure that the printer's printing machine lays out the text exactly as we think it is going to be laid out.

For example, for those who are planning to use the word-processing program Word to craft and typeset our prose, it is helpful to know that each printer prints a Word file slightly differently. This means that the sentence that ends one page might be found at the top of the next page when the Word file is printed on a different computer. It might be necessary to play around with page and printer settings to make sure that what is displayed on our computer screen and what is printed on the finished page is the same.

Indexes

Indexes are discussed in detail in *Writing Interesting Family Histories*. The most important information to know here is that, if we are self-publishing a family history, we shouldn't produce an index until after we have generated the pdf file because of the page-printing problems. If sentences end up on different pages, it will mess up our index.

Part 2: Publishing

There's a lot more to publishing a book
than writing it and
slapping a cover on it.

Vince Flynn

19

Publishing options

Mainstream publishing

When I thought about writing this book, I initially dismissed the idea of writing about mainstream publishing because family historians rarely succeed in obtaining mainstream publishing interest. Then I thought about my own writing/publishing experience and decided that it would be worthwhile briefly covering the subject in case other family historians find themselves in a similar situation.

Publisher

The term *publisher* has two meanings in the literary world. It refers to a publishing house; for example, Allen & Unwin, Penguin or PacMacmillan. It also refers to the in-house commissioning agent/ editor, the person within the publishing house who decides that your manuscript is worthy of merit and pitches it to the company's commissioning committee for funding.

Just as an aside, the computer file or print-out that contains our prose is called a *manuscript*. It does not become a *book* until it is published in either a hard-copy form or as an e-book.

One of the main differences between mainstream publishers and others is that mainstream publishers pay authors an advance against royalties. In Australia, advances were once five figures however they are usually smaller now for first-time authors because of the recent contraction of the publishing industry. Royalties are about 10% of the recommended retail price, but are lower internationally. Advances are paid in two or three parts. In my case, the first part of the advance is paid when the contract is signed, the second part when the manuscript is officially submitted, and the final part when the book is published. Most books don't pay out their advances so authors receive no further royalties.

A publisher acquires a manuscript for publication in one of three different ways: as an unsolicited manuscript, via a literary agent, or via a commission. These are discussed below.

Unsolicited manuscript

The pile of unsolicited manuscripts sent to a publisher is called a *slush pile*. The slush pile is about as close to a publisher's garbage bin as an eager writer can get. Mainstream publishers receive thousands of unsolicited manuscripts every year. Let's use an example of 5000, although this is probably closer to the number of fiction submissions alone.

The writer who has rigidly adhered to the submission guidelines for the particular publisher and has presented a professional looking and sounding covering letter on a topic that interests the publisher will likely make it through the first cut. At least 50% will be culled. Reasons for the culling include sending fiction manuscripts to a publishing house that refuses to accept unsolicited fiction, or sending manuscripts targeted at an adult audience to a publisher that publishes only children's books.

The submission guidelines (found on a publisher's website) include the layout of the manuscript: usually single white pages, double-spaced, ragged-edged, with a three-to-four centimetre margin and an eleven or twelve point font. I've heard of would-be authors printing and binding their manuscripts so that they look like a book. The publisher's attitude is that if the author can't be bothered finding out the guidelines and adhering to them, he or she doesn't deserve a contract. Any writer who is thinking about approaching a publisher, mainstream or otherwise, is strongly advised to invest in Noah Lukeman's *The First Five Pages* before doing so.

The first cull brings the number of manuscripts to be assessed down to 2500. Of these, 90% will be culled by the time the slush pile editor has read to the bottom of the first page and a further 8% by the end of the first chapter. This cull is primarily based on the prose: typographical errors, clichés, wooden prose, poorly structured sentences, switches of tense and point of view, and so on. This leaves around 50 submissions that will be assessed further. Approximately five of these will be published in any given year.

This means that a writer's odds of getting an unsolicited manuscript published is only one in five hundred. However, it is important to remember that the publishing industry is not a lottery. Publishers want new authors and are seeking original stories that are well-written and compelling. My first manuscript was picked up from the slush pile by the first publisher I approached in two weeks. It probably helped that I had 'true story' and 'sex scandal' in the first two sentences of my covering letter.

Literary agent

Most mainstream books are pitched to publishing companies by literary agents; however, it is even harder to obtain the services of a literary agent: around one in five-thousand. They only pick up authors who are likely to sell considerably more books than the average print-run so a good publishing track record is almost essential. In Australia, the average print-run is 3000 books and a best-seller is 10,000 books. The UK and US have much bigger publishing industries but they also have more would-be authors.

Commission

My first manuscript went into Allen & Unwin's slush-pile. My next four manuscripts were pitched by a literary agent, two after I wrote them and two as an idea for consideration. My sixth book was written under a commission.

Let me explain commissions by way of my own example. An independent publisher who works in with Allen & Unwin found a great true story and decided that I was the right author to write it. My response when I was approached was: 'I'd sell my soul for this story.' So they paid me to write it. Nice! That book is *Chubbie Miller*.

For most non-fiction books, a publisher sees a need within the community for a book on a certain subject and commissions an expert to write it. Alternatively, a high-profile figure is approached about writing an autobiography or working with a ghost-writer to do the same.

The family history genre

It is rare for a family history to gain the interest of a mainstream publisher or even an independent publisher (discussed below). Those that do are almost always written by historians rather than genealogists. Historians use a family's story as a vehicle to reflect the times and as a reflection of the times. They offer historical insight and enlightenment rather than simply documenting the facts. They analyse, narrate or use a combination of the two.

Occasionally, a family story – generally a single person's story – has the potential to be picked up by a publisher. I teach writing skills as part of Unlock the Past genealogical conferences on international cruise ships and a recent attendee told me that she is keen to write the story of one of her ancestors. This ancestor, Mary Gilbert, known as 'The Mother of Melbourne', had an interesting life story, not the least of which was her dramatic death in a house fire. As Melbourne is Australia's second largest city, the story has marketing potential. To be picked up by a publishing house, though, the prose must be of a high quality and the story itself needs to be much more than just a recitation of the facts of the woman's life.

To determine if a family history, or if an individual in the family, has a story that might attract the interest of a publisher, it is necessary to ask ourselves the following two questions. First: 'Am I a good enough writer that a publisher will choose my manuscript for publication instead of the other 499 manuscripts sitting in the slush pile?' Second: 'Is my story so interesting that 3000 people will be willing to pay $30 for a copy when they could spend that same $30 on any other book in the bookshop or at the movies or in a bar …?' When those questions are answered with an open mind, the answer is likely to be 'No.'

My own mainstream books are not family histories; they are true-crime thrillers. However, I discovered the stories at the heart of three of my six books when I was writing a family history. As most of my protagonists left descendants, these stories are family stories for these descendants. Thus, there are many family stories that are suitable for publication. They are better written as popular histories, though, than as family histories.

Other publishing options

There are a range of other publishing options which are discussed below.

Independent publishers

The publishing industry is pyramid-shaped as are so many other industries. As mentioned earlier, the top publishing companies pay the author an advance against royalties. The next level of publishing companies – which are generally referred to as the *independent* publishing companies – do not pay advances. They accept a manuscript, finance the publishing and printing costs, organise marketing and distribution, and pay the author a royalty on sales.

It is easier to get a book published by an independent publishing company because there are many more of them and they don't have to pay advances. However, the end result might not be what the author desired.

Vanity publishing

The difference between vanity publishing and self-publishing can seem confusing so vanity publishing will be explained by way of an example.

When I was a newbie author, I attended a seminar on book marketing and sat next to a woman who said that her fiction manuscript had been picked up by an American publisher. She had participated in an international sport and had written a thriller or romance centred on that sport. It all sounded rather exciting until the contract details gradually emerged.

Instead of being paid an advance on her book, she'd had to pay the publisher $14,000. For this sum, the company promised to edit, proof-read, cover design, typeset, print, market and distribute the book. She would get a certain number of books for free (50 or 100 from memory) and would get paid a 30% royalty on any sales.

As the details emerged, my alarm bells began ringing because I had read about vanity publishing. These companies make their money from the payments made by wannabe authors. They make a token effort at marketing and distributing a book. However, few newspapers or magazines send the books out for review because they know they are from a vanity publishing company. And few bookshops accept stock for the same reason. The publisher uses a print-on-demand system but there is no demand so few books are printed. Basically, for her $14,000, she would get 50 to 100 books and maybe, if she was lucky, a few hundred dollars in royalties.

Be warned.

Self-publishing

Self-publishing is different. Self-publishers – that is, us – are responsible for editing, proof-reading, cover design, typesetting, marketing and distribution of our books. We employ and pay a printer to print and bind our books. That's all. The next chapter covers self-publishing in detail.

E-books

The e-book market is huge and growing exponentially. Not only do mainstream and independent publishers publish their books in e-book form, millions of individuals use these mediums each year to publish their own books. In fact, most 'new books' are now self-published e-books.

E-book publishing is discussed further in the next chapter.

20

Self-publishing guide

The self-publishing big picture

After we have finished writing our manuscript, we need to prepare it for a printer. The 'find a printer' section is covered first because the service we buy dictates the amount of work we need to undertake to prepare our manuscript.

Find a printer

When I was looking for a printer for my Nash family history, I explored three options. I contacted a man who provides a full service for genealogists. He takes the Word file and all the images (pictures, maps, charts, etc.) and designs the layout, typesets the entire text, designs the cover, and prints and binds the book. It is a useful service for those who can afford it, but it was going to cost $75.00 per book in 2003 made worse by the fact that I would have to charge more to the purchasers (see 'Selling price' below).

I then obtained a quote from the Snap printing franchise. If I typeset the book myself (470 A4 pages) and designed the cover and sent them .pdf files for both, they would print and bind the book for $48.00 per book. It was more work for me but the purchase price would be much lower.

Someone recommended the printery at Charles Sturt University at Bathurst, New South Wales (a regional university). If I sent them the two pdfs, they would print and bind the books for $25.00 each. Needless to say, I typeset the books myself and sent the pdfs to Charles Sturt.

Since then I have produced a few additional small print-runs of the Nash family history, a dozen or half-a-dozen copies each. I used

Snap printery because they were close whereas I would have had to pay delivery costs from Charles Sturt, which is a few hours' drive from my home. The printing cost was horrendous and most family members have not wanted to pay the $99.50 purchase price. I won't produce any more.

So shop around. Check out the full-service providers, the local printeries and the printeries at regional universities.

For those who decide to typeset the books themselves, the necessary information is shown below. On first reading, it may seem overwhelming but it isn't. And remember, knowledge is always power.

Size and weight

It is important to think about the weight of our publication before we go much further. Most family histories will be posted to purchasers so, if we remain under weight barriers, it reduces the postage cost for purchasers which increases the purchasing appeal. Every country has different weight and size barriers. I will use the example of the Australian postal system as an example.

The Australian system allows us to post 'large letters' which are rectangular in shape, no larger than 260 mm x 360 mm and no thicker than 20 mm. The weight barriers (and current stamp costs) are 125 gm ($2), 250 gm ($3) and 500 gm ($5). This book falls into the 'large letter' category because it is A5 in size (148 x 210 mm), has a spine of 8 mm, and weighs under 250 grams.

When we post a book, we need to include the following in our postage calculations: the weight of the book, the weight of a covering letter or tax receipt, and the weight of the envelope.

Book weight: a perfect-bound book includes the paper, the cover and the glue. The total for this book is around 237 grams.

Paper: This book is A5 in size and the paper is 80 gsm (grams per square metre). There are 32 sheets of A5 paper in a square metre so each A5 sheet weights 2.5 grams (80 ÷ 32 = 2.5). This book is 140 pages in length, which means 70 sheets of A5 paper. The weight of the paper is therefore 70 x 2.5 = 175 grams.

Cover: This book has a 300 gsm cover so the front cover alone weighs about 9.4 grams (300 ÷ 32 = 9.4). The combined front cover, back cover and spine weigh about 20 grams.

Glue: The binding glue weighs about 40 grams.

Covering letter: If we include a single A4 page as a covering letter, it weighs 5 grams.

Envelope: A padded mailer (PB3: 215 x 280 mm) weighs 23 grams, which overshoots the 250 gram mark, so we are forced to use to a lighter envelope or reduce the number of pages.

How do we change the size of a book to keep it under the weight barriers? We have three options.

1. We reduce the font size and, correspondingly, the leading to reduce the number of pages in the book;
2. We adjust the margins to widen or lenghten the page slightly which allows more text on a single page; and/or
3. We tweak the text so we don't have a few words flowing onto a new page.

Note: We can only tweak a publication in this way if we undertake the typesetting ourselves. When changing the font size and adjusting the margins, remember the Golden Ratio (see 'Margins' below) and the number of characters per line (see 'Fonts' below).

ISBN

Make a point of obtaining an International Standardised Book Number (ISBN) for each book. This gets our book into 'the system' so descendants can easily find a reference to it. Google 'ISBN' and the relevant country to find out how to purchase one.

As an ISBN costs money, it is necessary to add the purchase price to the unit price of the book. If it costs $50 to buy the ISBN number and the print-run is 100 books, an additional 50 cents needs to be added to the selling price of each book.

It is unnecessary to obtain a barcode for a family history publication. However, it is a good idea to obtain a barcode for other self-published books such as this one. It is purchased by libraries and despatched through library suppliers.

Selling price

It is impossible to break even when we self-publish a book so we have two choices: we generate a profit or we suffer a loss. Since we have spent a huge amount of time and money researching and writing the family history, it is more than reasonable that we make a profit.

To determine the book price, we first add together the costs incurred in producing the book: cover design, book printing and binding, ISBN number, delivery costs and so on. Then we divide the total cost by the number of books to be printed to gain a unit publishing price for each book. So if we were printing 200 books at $25 per book (total $5000) and had additional costs of $50 for the cover design (discussed below) plus $50 for the ISBN plus $70 for delivery costs, the total is $5170. We divide this amount by the number of books being printed (200) and get a unit price of $25.85 per book.

A rule of thumb in self-publishing is to price a book at five times the unit publishing cost. This might seem an extraordinarily high mark-up; however, if the book is picked up by a distributor, the company will pay only 25-33% of the recommended retail price. Without a high mark-up, the author would make no money. Additionally, the author has to pay for stock in advance but might sit on copies for years. For instance, the first edition of *Writing Interesting Family Histories* took nine months to sell out but the second larger print-run took six years.

Most family history books cannot be priced anywhere near five times the unit publishing price. It would have been impossible to charge five times the $75.00 or $48.00 or even the $25.00 unit price for the Nash family history. Instead, I offered a pre-publication discount price of $49.50 (or $40.00 for close family members) and charged $69.50 once the book was published. The cost of four years of lost wages (I worked part-time) combined with the research and travel expenses I incurred would have easily topped $100,000 so the financial recompense from a few hundred books was negligible. However, for retirees with no demands on their time, a self-published family history could bring in some pocket-money.

Marketing

As soon as we start thinking about self-publishing a family history, we need to focus on building up an e-mail/address list of descendants who might be interested in purchasing the book. The larger the print-run, the cheaper the unit price of the book so it is best not to have hundreds of people coming out of the woodwork after we have published it.

Keep in contact with descendants by sending out a small e-mail newsletter every three to six months. This can be used to keep them abreast of discoveries, to ask for information about certain individuals, to alert them to the book's imminent publication and to advise them of a pre-publication discount offer. It will usually be necessary to access a bulk email sending program to send out the newsletter because our normal email servers prevent us from sending group emails. I pay for Sendblaster but other services are available for free.

Pre-publication discount offers are the best way to obtain an estimate of the size of the print-run. Make a point of printing more books than the pre-publication orders because word spreads after the book comes out so there will inevitably be additional orders. Pre-publication discount offers also bring in money to help cover the thousands of dollars that the print-run will probably cost.

Manuscript layout

Assuming that the decision is made to take responsibility for the entire self-publishing process, the following explains what a self-publisher needs to know.

Typesetting programs

Indesign is the professional typesetting program most book designers use. It costs a large annual fee so it is not an economic choice for one-off publications. I used Office's Publisher to produce the first two editions of *Writing Interesting Family Histories*. It – and Indesign for that matter – has a major flaw. It cannot cope with footnotes and endnotes. Seriously! Most of them were dumped as it converted the text from Word to Publisher. I ended up having to do most of them manually. This flaw might have been fixed in the years since, but check before you go too far.

The program Word can be tricky in terms of making photos stay in place, particularly in two-column publications. However, it is probably the best choice for a self-publishing beginner who is initially intent on producing a single family history.

White space

It is important that a book has plenty of white space, meaning that it has the appropriate blank pages, that the margins are not too small and cramped, that the line-spacing is not too narrow, and that the font is not too tight.

Double-page spread

When we write our family histories, we tend to see our text as a series of single A4 pages (or whatever page size we use). However, to effectively typeset our manuscript, we need to see it as a series of double-page spreads. Designing page layouts involves the aesthetic component as well as the practical. We'll examine all the relevant issues below.

Margins and binding

The outside margins of the two facing pages should be at least one centimetre (half-inch) in width, preferably two.

The top margin should be similar to the outside margin and should be slightly smaller than the bottom margin for aesthetic reasons (our eyes find it visually pleasing).

The size of the inside margin – or *gutter* – depends on the book binding. A *hard-cover* book with a *stitched* binding opens flat; therefore, some book designers consider that it is aesthetically more pleasing to have a narrower inside margin so the two facing pages of text look like they are parts of a whole. However, most family histories are not stitched. If the book is *perfect bound* (glued) or *stapled* or has a *spiral binding*, some of the inside margin is caught in the *spine*. That being the case, it is necessary to have a wider inside margin. It's best to add at least a centimetre or half-an-inch to whatever we have allowed for the outside margin if we want a perfect-bound book to appear as if the outside and inside margins are of the same size.

When determining the size of the margins, remember the Golden Ratio: the ratio of 1:1.6. If the width of the text block is considered to be 1, the height should be 1.6 times the width. This is helpful in determining the height-to-width ratio of the text-box and therefore, the size of the margins.

Fonts

It is important that we pick our fonts carefully. Most printed publications use a *serif* font, which means that it has little strokes added to the ends of letters. They are supposed to be easier to read in print. This text uses the basic Times New Roman font, which is a serif style. However, I have expanded the text slightly so it doesn't seem as cramped (see 'Letter spacing' below).

Most internet websites use *sans serif* fonts, those without the little strokes, as they are supposed to be easier to read on computer screens. My website uses Verdana.

It is considered aesthetically pleasing to use different font styles (serif, sans serif, etc.) for the chapter/subject headings as compared to the text however don't use too many different styles of font in the same publication. Two or three at a maximum. The chapter and subject headings of this book use the sans serif font Arial. The fonts used in this book are about as basic as they get. They didn't start that way. I found that the original fonts I chose while working with my Word file were not recognised by my typesetting program, Indesign. As I didn't have the time to learn how to get it to recognise fonts that weren't built into the system, it was easier to go with the basics.

It is important to also think about the point size of our font both in terms of aesthetics and readability. Too small is too difficult for older readers. Too large makes it seem like it is a 'Large Print' book for those with reading problems.

I once read that it is desirable to have about 70 characters of text in a single line for easy readability. This allows a single column of text in an A5 book. For an A4-sized family history, it is perhaps better to lay out the text in two columns otherwise each line will contain too many words.

For more information about page design and fonts, read Robin Williams' *The Non-Designer's Design Book.*

Setting up Word styles

Word's Home tab displays a series of pre-set styles. It saves us a lot of work if we use these styles for our headings and our main text (the 'Normal' style) and our quotes and so on. That way we don't have to manually change every paragraph if we decide to change the font size after we have started typesetting the book.

To change the style settings, right-click on the relevant style then choose 'Modify'. This brings up a box that allows us to change the font, point-size and so on. If we want to change anything else, click 'Format' on the bottom-left of the 'Modify Style' box and choose the relevant option.

Letter-spacing

In the old days of dot-matrix printers, each letter took up the same amount of space which produced a stilted and gappy effect. Today's printers use proportional spacing, such that narrow letters like 'i' take up less room than broad letters like 'm'.

We have the ability to change the spacing between words and letters if we feel that a line looks too cramped or if we want to narrow the spacing so that, for example, a word at the end of a chapter doesn't go across to a new page (every page costs us money). To do so, highlight the relevant sentence (or paragraph) and make sure the Home tab is displayed at the top of the screen. The current Word program has a number of blocks of information in the full-size menu at the top of the screen: Clipboard (to the left), Font, Paragraph, Styles and so on. Click the arrow box to the right of 'Font' then click the 'Advanced' tab. Our options are listed under 'Character spacing'. We can 'Scale' it by a percentage or we can choose one of the 'Spacing' options: 'Expanded' or 'Condensed'.

We have the same options in our 'Normal' style as well, if we want to tighten or loosen the text in our entire manuscript.

Line-spacing or leading

Pronounced 'ledding', this refers to the spacing between the base-lines of our text. In the old days, *leading* was a thin strip of lead that was used to increase the space between the lines of type. Otherwise, one row of type would have sat directly on top of the following row.

Most of us think about the line-spacing of our text in terms of single-spacing and double-spacing. The word-processing program Word formerly defaulted to single-spacing, but now defaults to 1.15 spacing. The desirable leading is 20% larger than the font height, meaning that 1.20 would technically be better than 1.15, however single-spacing (1.0) already has some inbuilt leading.

How do we change line-spacing? To explore the spacing options, click on the up-and-down arrows in the Paragraph box on the Home tab. It will bring up a box listing '1.0, 1.15, 1.5, 2.0' and so on. Click the 'line spacing options' and it will bring up an options screen. Go to the 'Spacing' section and find the 'Line spacing' option and choose 'Multiple'. In the neighbouring 'At' box, we can type in the amount of line-spacing we want: 1.00 (single-spacing), 1.15, 1.20, and so on. Play around with the amount until it looks aesthetically pleasing and easy to read – not too cramped, not too spread out.

We can also get to the same screen by clicking on the little arrow box to the right of 'Paragraph' on the full-screen menu.

It is a good idea to use the 'Styles' option to set the line-setting for all of our text. To change the font and spacing, right-click on Normal and choose 'Modify'. Then click Format on the bottom-left and choose 'Paragraph'. The same 'Paragraph' box will come up. Whatever we choose on that screen will affect all of our Normal text. When we use the Style options for headings, quotes and so on, we have consistent styles throughout our publications and consistent changes if we want to change them.

Paragraph layout

Have a look at the paragraph layout in this book. There are no gaps between paragraphs (except when information is quoted) and the first line of each paragraph is indented a short distance (except at the start of a chapter or section). This is the paragraph layout used for most professionally published books and is the most desirable layout for a family history. It is easy-to-read, it doesn't waste money by wasting space, and the text flows naturally.

The Word program defaults to block paragraphs – those with no indentation and a line-break between paragraphs. Do not use this style for a family history or a journal or anything else. It creates a jerky feel and wastes space. In fact, it can add many unnecessary pages to a publication.

The worst design is the block paragraph style with indented paragraphs. It looks as if each paragraph is drifting in white space.

To change the paragraph layout in our 'Normal' style, follow the instructions in the last paragraph of the previous section to get to the 'Paragraph' screen. To produce a layout similar to this book, change the 'Before' and 'After' spacing options to '0'. In the Indentation section on the same screen, go to the 'Special' option and choose 'First Line'. In the 'By' box, choose the amount. This book has a first-line indentation of 0.4 cm.

Apart from the first line in any chapter or section, the only other paragraphs that do not have an indented first line are those that continue the same idea but have been interrupted by the intrusion of a quote or picture or map.

Front pages

Have a look at the front pages of this book to get an idea of what is needed. The title page must always be on a right-hand page. Sometimes it is the first page of a book. If it is not the first page, it must never be the second (left) page.

Sometimes the first page includes author information – as this book does. It is a good idea to have information about the author somewhere in the book. Readers like to know about the person who wrote it.

The back of the author information page is a good place to provide details of other publications by the same author – as this book does. More detailed information about some or all of the author's publications can be included at the back of the book if there is room.

On the back of the title page (called the back-title page or imprint page), the publishing details are listed. Use the details on the back-title page of this book as a guide for a self-published book. I extracted them from one of my mainstream-published books.

Contents page

The contents page is always a right-hand page. Sometimes it will continue onto a second or third or fourth page. Whatever its length, the next section should always start on a right-hand page.

Main text

The first page of a book's text should start on a right-hand page. In this book, the first page of text is the section page headed 'Part 1: Writing'. Ideally, the first chapter that follows this section heading should also start on a right-hand page. Occasionally, page limitations prevent this, as is the case with this book.

Some books always start a new chapter on a right-hand page. This is unnecessary and wastes space. However, a new section page (eg. 'Part 2: Publishing') should always start on a right-hand page.

It is always a good idea to tweak the manuscript during the typesetting process to ensure that it doesn't have headings on the bottom line of a page or a single line on the last page of a chapter. There are three ways to tweak a manuscript.

1. Rewrite any paragraphs in the chapter that end with only a word or two on a new line. This might be enough to pull that last line onto the previous page;
2. Allow hyphenation of long words. Again, this might be enough to reduce the number of lines in that or a previous paragraph; and/or
3. Tweak the letter spacing or word spacing for a paragraph or a series of paragraphs.

Make a point of proof-reading a manuscript before it is typeset and afterwards as well because the tweaking process can lead to errors. In fact, read a manuscript through as many times as possible to try to reduce the number of errors. Some will inevitably slip through, even with the help of professionals.

End pages

Most family histories will have endnotes, a bibliography and an index (and, of course, annotated timelines). These are discussed in *Writing Interesting Family Histories*.

Cover design

The first two editions of *Writing Interesting Family Histories* had self-designed covers, which were ordinary to say the least. The problem was that I didn't know how to find a professional designer who could produce a cover design without charging a fortune. The price of the cover design needs to be divided between the number of books printed and added to the unit price of each book. For example, if a cover design costs $500 and we print 200 copies of our family history, we are adding $2.50 to the unit publishing price for each book.

I have now found an affordable cover designer through the website fiverr.com. Have you heard of this website? It acts as an intermediary between those who need a service and those willing to provide one for $5. Of course, it costs a lot more than $5 to purchase the design for a book's full cover (front, spine and back) but it is only a fraction of the local price.

My book-cover designer is brilliant and his details are on the back-title page. However, there are others offering their services who are neither as able nor as honest. I once attempted to buy a different service through fiverr.com but the result was unusable.

When we send the cover details to a designer, we need to provide the following: size of publication (A5 for this book which is 148mm x 210mm), number of pages or sheets of paper (make it clear which is being specified as this determines spine width), title, author name, blurb, author information, ISBN barcode (if purchased), website address (if relevant) and the book's category (History/Family History).

I made the mistake of putting a price on the cover design of earlier editions. Avoid this because a price hike might prove necessary if a smaller second or third print-run is published at a more expensive price.

Self-publishing assistance

The explosion in self-publishing has led to the need for self-publishing assistance: editing, proofreading, cover design, the works. Service providers include Createspace, a division of Amazon.com. Using these services will add a hefty cost to the unit publishing price but, if there is no one else to help, the cost might be worth it.

I have used Createspace to upload copies of my 'how to' manuscripts for its international print-on-demand services. I regularly receive cheques for books sold via Amazon.com, Barnes & Noble and so on, which are sent to me in US dollars, minus the IRS withholding tax. I do not have an American bank account so bank charges are hefty. The books themselves require international postage if they are sent to Australian purchasers. Thus, this printing option is better for genealogists who are writing books in, say, America or the United Kingdom for local audiences and for which Amazom.com will send cheques in the local currency.

Uploading books to Createspace is an automated process that requires time and patience, particularly as it does not offer the option of book sizes based on the metric measurement system (A5, A4 and so on). Thus, the text has to be converted to a different book size. I won't go into the specifics here but will write a newsletter article that discusses the topic.

If images are included – photographs, maps, charts – they are often rejected by the uploading program. Getting it to accept an image-filled text would be a huge exercise in itself and would require the patience of a saint.

Converting a manuscript into an e-book

Once the text is uploaded to Createspace, it can then be converted into an e-book. This also takes an extraordinary amount of time and patience. I haven't got around to doing this for any of my recent 'how to' books because I haven't had the time. I doubt if I ever will for *Help! Why can't I find my ancestor's surname?* because it has 220 charts that would need to be manually dealt with. Again, I won't go into the specifics of the conversion process here but will write a newsletter article on the subject.

Conclusion

If I could provide a single piece of advice to help you craft a gripping family history, it is this:

Don't stop at 'what'.

Seek the 'why' and the 'how'.

Most genealogists are delighted to find the 'what' – the reference to an ancestor in a church record, census, military return, land dealing, and so on. The 'what' is so precious to them, because it was so hard to find, that it becomes the genealogical equivalent of gold. Accordingly, these genealogists think that the 'what' is all that matters. And that's all they include in their family histories.

Those who have reached the next level often focus much of their time and energy on the analysis of the evidence associated with the 'what'. They write family histories that are filled with the 'what', the evidence-analysis of the 'what', and the occasional chunks of background information. The latter are intended to communicate 'why' but are often little more than different varieties of 'what'.

These genealogists rarely think seriously about the 'how and the 'why'. Why is this record being kept? Why is my ancestor listed in it? Why did my ancestor do whatever he (or she) did that led him to be listed in it? How did he do whatever he did? Why did my ancestor's society develop in such a way that he did what he did? How are my ancestor's actions a reflection of that society and its development? And so on.

Clearly, you are not among these genealogists – or you won't be for long – because you are seeking ways to write gripping family histories. To do so, it is critical that you re-evaluate not only your writing process but your research focus. The 'what' should merely be the stepping stone in your search for the more interesting 'how' and 'why'. To find the 'how' and 'why', you will need to undertake extensive background research on the times, on the event itself, and on human nature. When you use the story-telling strategies discussed in this book – that is, structure, point of view, direction, tension, sensory information and so on – to communicate the 'what', the 'how' and the 'why', you are well on your way to writing a gripping family history.

But if I am allowed to offer a second piece of advice, it would be this. Read *narrative non-fiction* – that is, non-fiction told as a story – which is the official term for my own mainstream writing genre. I cannot stress this enough so I will repeat it:

READ NARRATIVE NON-FICTION

If you want to write a gripping family history, STOP reading other family histories. The best that can be said of most of them is that they are examples of what NOT to do.

Instead, immerse yourself in narrative non-fiction. It is impossible to truly grasp how to write gripping non-fiction unless you read lots of gripping non-fiction.

The narrative non-fiction books mentioned in this publication are in the reading list on the next page. Read them. Be inspired by them. Be inspired not only by the stories they tell but by the way the authors craft their stories. Then use the strategies discussed in this book to help you craft your own stories.

In this book and its companion volume, *Writing Interesting Family Histories*, I not only *tell* you the 'what', I *show* you the 'how' and the 'why'. Now it's up to you.

Enjoy the journey.

Reading List

Writing Books

Bernhardt, William *Sizzling Style: Every Word Matters* (Kindle e-book) and all his other writing books

Buckham, Mary *Writing Active Setting: The Complete How-To Guide* (Kindle e-book) and all her other writing books

Hall, Rayne *Writing Vivid Descriptions* (Kindle e-book) and all her other writing books

Kennedy, Marcy *Point of View in Fiction* (Kindle e-book) and all her other writing books

Kovalin, Val *How to Write Descriptions of Eyes and Faces* and *How to Write Descriptions of Hair and Skin* (Kindle e-books)

Narrative non-fiction

Annear, Robin *The man who lost himself: The unbelievable story of the Tichborne claimant*, 2002
(A fascinating Victorian legal cause célèbre.)

Brown, Daniel James *The Boys In the Boat: An Epic Journey to the Heart of Hitler's Berlin*, 2013
(A lyrical tale of a group of American Olympic-winning rowers.)

Sobell, Dava *Longitude: The True Story of the Lone Genius who Solved the Greatest Scientific Problem of His Time*, 1995
(A beautiful tale of a discovery that helped save our ancestors' lives.)

Winchester, Simon *The Surgeon of Crowthorne: A Tale of Murder, Madness and the Making of the Oxford English Dictionary*, 1998; also called *The Professor and the Madman*
(Wonderful!)

Index

Carol Baxter's 'how to' books

Writing Interesting Family Histories

Keen to write an engaging family history? Stuck with little more than names and dates? Uncertain how to begin? *Writing INTERESTING Family Histories* is a must-read. With advice ranging from how you can structure a simple family history and begin writing, through to how you can use simple words and sentences to evoke drama and tension, this book will help turn your dusty piles of notes and photocopies into a riveting family history. There is no need to fictionalise history to make it interesting! After reading this book, you too will be able to turn dry facts into exciting narrative.

Help! Historical and Genealogical Truth: How do I separate fact from fiction?

We sit at our computer searching for information about our ancestors and ... click ... we find something new and intriguing. But it contradicts something else we've found. HELP!

This book is a 'must-read' for family history detectives wishing to accurately trace their ancestry. It explains how to evaluate our ancestral information so as to determine which is reliable and which is like a virus that corrupts our efforts. After reading this book, you too will be able to separate fact from fiction, truth from mistruth.

Help! Why can't I find my ancestor's surname?

How often have you sat looking at a historical register or in front of a computer screen expecting to see your ancestor's surname only to discover that it's not there? You check every spelling you can think of without success then give up the search unaware that the entry is there but that you lack enough knowledge about letters and sounds to find it.

This book is the solution to your problem. It describes the distortions that can occur between the time your ancestor thought about saying his or her surname to the time you search for the surname. And it provides guidelines you can follow to help find those elusive surnames. When you follow its instructions, you will find that some of those previously abandoned surname searches are now successful.

www.carolbaxter.com

Carol Baxter's popular histories

An Irresistible Temptation: the true story of Jane New and a colonial scandal. Set between 1829 and 1834, it tells the story of a sex scandal that rocked New South Wales and contributed to Britain's decision to recall the governor. It is set against the backdrop of the progressive versus conservative attitudes in a society that was struggling to throw off its penal settlement shackles.

Breaking the Bank: an extraordinary colonial robbery. Set in 1828, it tells the story of Australia's largest ever bank robbery. Convicts in the penal settlement tunnelled through a sewerage drain and into the vault of the 'gentlemen's bank' stealing the equivalent, in today's terms, of about $20 million. It is set against the backdrop of the upstairs/downstairs politics of New South Wales.

Captain Thunderbolt and His Lady: the true story of bushrangers Frederick Ward and Mary Ann Bugg. Set in the 1860s, it tells the story of Australia's 'gentleman bushranger', who was on the run from the police for nearly seven years, and his part-Aboriginal lover. It is set against the backdrop of a 'people versus the establishment' period of political and social dissent.

The Peculiar Case of the Electric Constable: a true tale of passion point and pursuit. The electric telegraph was the first commercial use of electricity. The technology was struggling commercially until New Year's Day 1845 when it was used to apprehend a murder suspect, the protagonist of this story. The consequences kick-started the Communication Revolution.

Black Widow: the true story of Australia's first female serial killer. Set in 1888/89, it tells the story of Australia's first female serial killer and is set against the backdrop of women's rights and capital punishment.

Chubbie Miller: the Australian aviator and adventure who beguiled the world. Set during the Golden Age of Aviation (1927-1932) it tells the story of a feisty Australian woman who become one of America's top female aviators. It is a story of adventure, drama, mystery and tragedy.

Made in the USA
Las Vegas, NV
30 October 2022

58439546R00079